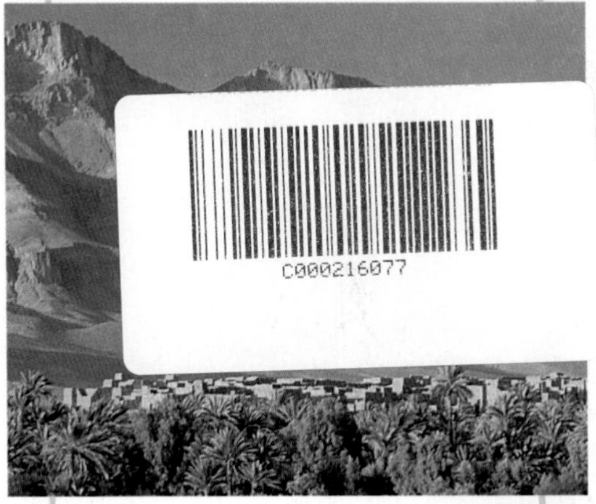

Essential Morocco

by Anthony Sattin and Sylvie Franquet

Sylvie Franquet studied Arabic at the universities of Ghent, Tunis and Cairo, and lived in Cairo for six years, working as a model, translator and tour manager. She writes a column for the Belgian newspaper *De Morgen*. Anthony Sattin is a regular contributor to the *Daily Telegraph* and *Sunday Times*, and has also written a novel, *Shooting the Breeze*, and *Lifting the Veil*, a history of travellers and tourists in Egypt from 1768 to 1956.

Together they have written AA *Explorer Egypt* and the *Greek Islands*, and AA *CityPack Bangkok*, and *Brussels & Bruges*.

AA Publishing

Above: *children are royalty in Morocco*

Page 1: *one of the Dra Valley's fortified* ksour

Page 5a: *a blue man in the Merzouga sand dunes*
5b: *Meknès family*

Page15a: *Chechaouen*
15b: *typical pottery*

Page 27a: *El-Jadida's medina*
27b: *snake-charmers*

Page 91a: *Royal Mansour Hotel, Moroccan buffet*
91b: *waterseller*

Page 117a: *coppersmith*
117b: *camels for sale*

Find out more about AA Publishing and the wide range of services the AA provides by visiting our Web site at www.theaa.co.uk.

Written by Anthony Sattin and Sylvie Franquet

Edited, designed and produced by AA Publishing.

Reprinted Apr and Nov 1998; Reprinted Apr 1999

Distributed in the United Kingdom by AA Publishing, Norfolk House, Priestley Road, Basingstoke, Hampshire, RG24 9NY.

A CIP catalogue record for this book is available from the British Library.

ISBN 0 7495 1633 X

We have tried to ensure accuracy in this guide, but things do change and we would be grateful if readers would advise us of any inaccuracies they may encounter.

Published by AA Publishing, a trading name of Automobile Association Developments Limited, whose registered office is Norfolk House, Priestley Road, Basingstoke, Hampshire, RG24 9NY.
Registered number 1878835.

Colour separation: BTB Digital Imaging Ltd, Whitchurch, Hampshire

Printed and bound in Italy by Printers Trento srl

Contents

About this Book

KEY TO SYMBOLS

Throughout the guide a few straightforward symbols are used to denote the following categories:

- map reference to the maps in the What to See section
- address or location
- telephone number
- opening times
- restaurant or café on premises or near by
- nearest underground train station
- nearest bus/tram route
- nearest overground train station
- nearest ferry stop
- travel by air
- tourist information
- facilities for visitors with disabilities
- admission charge
- other places of interest near by
- other practical information
- ➤ indicates the page where you will find a fuller description

Essential *Morocco* is divided into five sections to cover the most important aspects of your visit to Morocco.

Viewing Morocco pages 5–14
An introduction to Morocco by the authors
Morocco's Features
Essence of Morocco
The Shaping of Morocco
Peace and Quiet
Morocco's Famous

Top Ten pages 15–26
The authors' choice of the Top Ten places to see in Morocco, with practical information.

What to See pages 27–90
The four main areas of Morocco, each with its own brief introduction and an alphabetical listing of the main attractions.
Practical information
Snippets of 'Did You Know...' information
4 suggested walks
4 suggested tours
2 features

Where To... pages 91–116
Detailed listings of the best places to eat, stay, shop, take the children and be entertained.

Practical Matters pages 117–24
A highly visual section containing essential travel information.

Maps
All map references are to the individual maps found in the What to See section of this guide.
For example, Tizi-n-Test has the reference 72C2 – indicating the page on which the map is located and the grid square in which the pass is to be found. A list of the maps that have been used in this travel guide can be found in the index.

Prices
Where appropriate, an indication of the cost of an establishment is given by **£** signs:
£££ denotes higher prices, **££** denotes average prices, while **£** denotes lower charges.

Star Ratings
Most of the places described in this book have been given a separate rating:

- ✪✪✪ Do not miss
- ✪✪ Highly recommended
- ✪ Worth seeing

Viewing Morocco

Our Morocco

Breaking Down the Walls
As visitors, we become used to crenellated walls surrounding Morocco's old towns. New Moroccan architecture also tends to be surrounded by high walls. It should come as no surprise, therefore, that many Moroccan's have something of a 'wall mentality' which expresses itself as a curiosity but also a suspicion of strangers. Happily it doesn't usually take much to bring the walls down.

Morocco is known as Maghreb el Aksa, the land of the far west, which describes its place in the Arab world and also in Africa. Being distant from the centre of Arab culture and politics seems to suit the Moroccan identity. Like their language, which is an idiosyncratic dialect of Arabic, their customs, their attitudes and their view on the world is all their own.

There is great variety in the Moroccan character, from the sophistication of Fassis and the cosmopolitan outlook of Tangerinos to the wildness of southern Berbers and impermiability of mountain-hardened Atlas people. But in every region, Moroccans live up to their reputation for hospitality: when a guest is invited home, tables are never empty and when they meet in the street, they take time for proper greetings. Moroccans are also devoutly religious, led by a king who claims descent from the Prophet Muhammad and who carries the title Commander of the Faithful.

The French controlled Morocco from 1912–56, a short span in Morocco's long history but, coming at a time of great international and technological advances, one which has left its mark. The French built new towns (*villes nouvelles*) alongside the traditional Moroccan medinas, which has resulted in most towns and cities having a dual character. For the visitor this can mean walking from a place which looks like something out of an Arabian Nights fantasy into a reflection of provincial France. In the countryside, dotted with the tombs of *marabouts* (saints), a more fundamental and spiritual influence is felt.

A visit to the mosque is very much part of everyday life in the medina

Morocco's Features

Changing landscape: from the lush Ourika valley to the snowcapped Atlas Mountains

Moroccans

There are 28 million Moroccans, of whom almost 2 million live abroad. Over half are under 20, with many people living below the poverty line. Some 40 per cent of Moroccans work on the land, although that number is shrinking as more people move to towns and cities.

Language

Arabic, in a dialect quite distinct in sound from classical Arabic, is most widely spoken, although 40 per cent of Moroccans still speak one of the thousand Berber languages as their first language. Some Moroccans descended from Arabs who fled Spain in the 15th century still speak Spanish (mostly in the north), as do people living in the Spanish enclave of Ceuta. Many people, particularly in urban areas, also speak French, a legacy of colonisation.

Landscape

There is a great variety of landscape in Morocco, including: 3,500km of coastline; plenty of mountains including Jbel Toubkal, the highest in North Africa; lush farmland, steppe, the Sahara desert and its oases, home to around 5 million palm trees.

Economy

Farming is the mainstay of the Moroccan economy. Morocco has one of the world's largest phosphate deposits, which accounts for some 25 per cent of total export revenue. Textiles, leather and fish are the other three main export items. In 1995, tourism earned almost as much as phosphate exports.

Essence of Morocco

As a country which boasts of snowcapped mountains and sandy deserts, fertile plains and long white beaches, ancient ruins and modern resorts, Morocco has plenty to offer visitors. Its main cities include exotic Marrakech and the world's best-preserved medieval Arab medina, Fès, the beautiful bastion of Essaouira on the Atlantic coast, and blue-painted Chechaouen with its echoes of Andalucia in the Rif Mountains. South of Marrakech, whether in the High Atlas valleys or down in the Sahara, the great kasbahs and palm cultivations are an inspiration. Further south, the great emptiness of the Sahara is waiting to be explored.

THE 10 ESSENTIALS

There are a thousand and one things you could do in Morocco, but be sure not to leave the country without having tried the following:

- **Drink mint tea** – short, sweet and full of leaves, this is *the* drink of Morocco.
- **Bargain in the souk.** It's an art Moroccans learn from birth, but it's never too late to start...
- **Watch the moon through palm trees.** In the gardens of a grand hotel, like La Mamounia in Marrakech or the Palais Jamai in Fès, or down in a desert palmerie, what could be more romantic?
- **Eat a typical Moroccan meal.** Prepare yourself beforehand because as star chef Boujemaa Mars (Le Marocain Restaurant, Marrakech, ➤ 101) admits, 'there is no light *cuisine* in Morocco.' Traditional dishes tend to challenge the waistline while delighting the tastebuds.
- **Listen to Moroccan music** in the Jemaa el-Fna in Marrakech (➤ 19) or a theme restaurant in Tangier (➤ 31–5). The rhythms will be familiar from Flamenco music, but the sound is unique.
- **See the Atlas Mountains.** North Africa's highest mountains are the country's centrepiece, with thrilling landscape, fresh air, extraordinary architecture and friendly Berber people.
- **Visit a medersa.** Most mosques in Morocco are closed to non-Muslims, but some medersas (Koran schools) are open and, as in Fès (➤ 20), Meknès (➤ 65) and Marrakech (➤ 75) are beautifully decorated.

- **See a traditional house** (even if it is has been converted into a shop or restaurant). Sumptuous pleasures behind austere walls.
- **Walk through a medina without a guide.** Run the risk of getting lost for the pleasure of being in the old towns and their inhabitants without an intermediary.
- **Feel the sand beneath your feet.** Desert or beach, Morocco has plenty of it.

Above: *traders in disguise and sweet mint tea are all part of buying a carpet*

Opposite: *waterseller in Rabat*

Bottom: *the walls of Marrakech at sunset*

Below: *each alley in the medina hides other delights and treasures*

The Shaping of Morocco

c1000 BC
Phoenician traders established posts and colonies at Tanger and along the Atlantic coast.

25 BC
King Juba II ruled as a Roman 'client-king'. Purple dye from the islands off Essaouira was exported to Rome.

AD 44
Mauritania, as Morocco was then known, was absorbed into the Roman Empire with Volubilis as its capital.

c AD 285
Roman legions pulled back to the Mediterranean coast, leaving the former colony to the Berbers and later to the Vandals and Byzantines.

The local holy man preaching war against the French was sure of a large attendance

682
Oqba Ibn Nafi led an Arab army from Tunisia to Morocco. Twenty years later another Muslim army arrived. In 711, the conquest of Spain began.

Idrissids (788–923)
789
Fès was founded by Moulay Idriss, descendant of the Prophet Muhammad. The previous year he had been acknowledged *imam* (religious leader) of the Berber tribes. He was the first to unite northern Morocco after the Roman retreat.

792
Idriss II became sultan after his father was poisoned by agents of the Baghdad caliph Haroun er-Rachid. Fès became the new capital.

Almoravids (1062–1145)
1042
Youssef Ibn Tachfine, a Berber leader from southern Morocco, established a new capital and a new dynasty – the Almoravids – at Marrakech in 1070. In 1086, he invaded Spain. The Almoravid Koubba in Marrakech is cited as the prototype of Moroccan decoration.

Almohads (1147–1248)
1147
In response to the new reformist message of Ibn Tumert of Tin-Mal, the Almohads (unitarians), a confederation of Atlas Berbers, conquered Marrakech. Under Yacoub el Mansour (1184–99), Moroccan fleets controlled the

western Mediterranean and Marrakech was the centre of an empire which included Spain, Algeria and Tunisia.

Merenids (1248–1465)
1269
The Beni-Merin Berbers rose against the Almohads, killed the sultan in Marrakech and established their own Merenid dynasty.

1331
The accession of Abou Hassan (1331–51) marked the start of the high point of Merenid rule. His son Abou Inan (1351–58) developed Fès Jdid and built the great medersas in Fès and Meknès.

Saadians (1554–1669)
1578
Following the Battle of the Three Kings near Asilah, the victorious Saadian ruler Ahmed el Mansour took control of West Africa's gold mines, earning himself the name Eddahabi, the Golden One, and building the Badia palace in Marrakech with the proceeds.

Alaouites (since 1669)
1672
Moulay Ismail inherited the sultanate and ruled ruthlessly and effectively until 1727, building the Imperial City in Meknès.

The Moroccan Crown Prince: does he represent the real future of Morocco?

1764
Sidi Mohammed Ben Abdullah encouraged Morocco's foreign trade links by making the newly-fortifying Essaouira a major port.

1912
Morocco became a French protectorate, with Spain receiving control of parts of the north. French governor Lyautey made Rabat his centre and constructed '*villes nouvelles*' alongside Moroccan medinas.

1956
Sidi Mohammed ben Youssef became King Mohammed V as Morocco received independence from France and Spain after years of violent struggle.

1962
Hassan II succeeded his father. Morocco's first political elections were held the following year.

1975
King Hassan II encouraged the 'Green March', in which some 350,000 Moroccan citizens walked south to occupy the former Spanish Sahara, opposed by the Algerian-backed Polisario group, who wanted an independent Western Sahara. The quest to find an acceptable, UN-recognised solution continues.

1990–1
Morocco sent a number of troops to fight with the US-led coalition in Kuwait against Iraq.

Peace & Quiet

Moroccan towns and cities are growing fast as the population increases and more people leave the countryside in search of better-paid work. But if you feel in need of escape, the country is never far away, with a great choice of landscape in which to relax.

The Desert

So many people head for the desert's open spaces in search of solitude that sometimes you won't be alone. As well as people, you'll find a surprising variety of birds and other animals. Near Ouarzazate, the El Mansour Eddahabi reservoir attracts flocks of migrating birds, as do the Todra and Dadès gorges. Following the Todra or Draa rivers south, you don't have to stray far from the road to be surrounded by desert (and don't even think of leaving the road without a four-wheel drive and either experience or a guide). Alternatively, the desert oases and palm groves offer a remarkable sense of calm.

The pretty orange tip butterfly is a frequent sight in the higher Atlas gorges

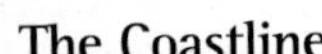

The Coastline

Only part of Morocco's 3,500km of coastline has been developed, so it is still possible to find stretches of untouched shore: between Agadir and Essaouira, for instance, and south of Agadir. Some of the best bird-watching coastline is Cap Blanc near Oualidia, Cap Rhir near Agadir and the coast around Tanger.

Inland

Just inland from the coast there are a number of spots worth travelling to. Imouzzer-Ida has some startlingly beautiful landscape and waterfalls. The reedbeds of Sidi Bourhaba lake near Mehdiya attract a wide variety of birds. The Mardja Zerga lake, on the Moulay-Bousselham Reserve further north, attracts serious birdwatchers in winter to see the endangered slender-billed curlew.

Mountain Ranges

The High Atlas mountains present a range of possibilities. The landscape is a tonic in itself, the valleys among Morocco's most beautiful attractions – particularly in spring. Should you need more, there is a variety of birds, including birds of prey, rare butterflies, unusual flora and the snowcapped peaks to cool your mind.

The more gentle contours of the Middle Atlas and Rif Mountains contain some beautiful forests and lakes. In the

Above: *storks build their nests on top of Roman temples and houses or high up in the trees*

Middle Atlas, lakes ('dayets') Aaoua, Hacklaf, Ifrah and Aguelmam Azigza provide excellent bird-watching opportunities, there are impressive cedar woods and other forests around Ifrane, Azrou and Midelt, while the reservoir Bin el Ouidane is a centre for hunting: if you're not into bloodsports, the nearby Cascades d'Ouzoud waterfall will calm your spirit.

Gardens

Finally don't forget that Morocco is famous for its gardens, from the Jardins Exotiques at Bouknadel to the extraordinary 18th-century garden of the Mamounia Hotel, Marrakech, worth the price of an excellent coffee to explore. Elsewhere, ignoring the secrets hidden behind medina walls, which few of us will ever see, horticultural pleasures are on offer at the Dar Batha Museum and Palais Jamaï Hotel (Fès), the Dar el Makhzen and Palais Mendoub (Tanger), kasbah of Chechaouen, Chella and Musée des Arts Marocains (Rabat), Dar Jamaï Museum (Meknès), the Menara and Aguedal Garden, Marrakech, and Majorelle's garden, restored by Yves St. Laurent and victim of its own success, and many, many more.

A Birdwatcher's Guide to Morocco by Patrick and Fedora Bergier has more detailed information on bird sites.

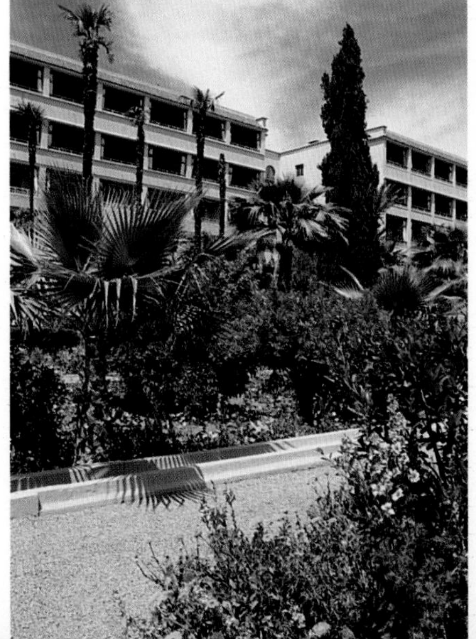

Left: *the well-tended gardens of the legendary Mamounia Hotel in Marrakech*

Morocco's Famous

HRH King Hassan II
Images of the reigning king, Commander of the Faithful, descended from the Prophet Muhammad, are common throughout the kingdom. On 3 March, the anniversary of the king's accession, there are widespread celebrations. Outside Morocco, King Hassan II is credited with helping his country to avoid the divisions which have overtaken neighbouring Algeria and for his firm stand on the Gulf War and the Middle East peace talks.

HRH King Mohammed V

The third-born son, Sidi Mohammed was chosen by the French to succeed his father Sultan Moulay Youssef in 1927 and was crowned king on independence in 1956.

Said Aouita

Aouita has been a leading figure in world athletics since winning an Olympic gold medal in the 5,000m in 1984.

Tahar Ben Jelloun

Morocco's most famous writer, living in Paris but writing very much in a Moroccan idiom, mixing beautiful dreams with a harsh reality.

Eugene Delacroix

Travelling with a French royal delegation in 1832, Delacroix was struck by the inaccuracy of the image of Morocco and Moroccans presented by previous artists and writers. In response, he created some of the 19th-century's greatest paintings.

Ibn Battuta

Born in Tanger in 1304, often described as 'the Arab Marco Polo', Ibn Battuta travelled to India and China before returning to Fès to write about his experiences.

Ibn Khaldun

The great Arab historian, born in Tunis in 1322, was long-time ambassador to the court of Fès. In the *Muqaddimah*, his introduction to the history of the world, Ibn Khaldun was the first person to write about the patterns of history.

Moulay Idriss

Descendant of the Prophet Muhammad, Idriss fled Damascus in 787 and was welcomed as spiritual leader at Volubilis, then northern Morocco's main city. He was poisoned in 792 on orders of the Baghdad caliph, having founded Fès, and Morocco's first Arab dynasty.

General Lyautey

The first Resident General of the French Protectorate is considered one of the founding fathers of modern Morocco and was originally buried in Rabat, the city he made capital.

Top Ten

1
Chechaouen

29E6

11km east of Tanger

Kasbah daily 10–noon, 2–dusk

Grills and cafés in Uta el Hammam (£) and restaurants in Hotel Parador (££)

CTM from Tanger, Ouezzane. Meknès, Tetouan, Al-Hoceima. Grand Taxis to Tetouan, Ouezzane

Kasbah: none

Kasbah: cheap

Tetouan (➤ 42, 43)

Small whitewashed Chechaouen, sitting 600m above the sea in the Rif mountains, is a town of tradition, mystery and calm.

Founded in 1471 to stop Spanish and Portuguese forces from moving inland, Chechaouen (also known as Chaouen) fiercely maintained its independence until the Spanish army broke into town in 1920. Before then, only two Christians had ever visited Chechaouen and lived to tell the tale. The Berber tribes, who mixed with Moors fleeing from Andalucia after the fall of Granada (1492), still have a strong sense of their separate identity.

The medina is accessible and enjoyable. It's also small enough to see without a guide; if you lose your way it won't belong before you find your way out. Houses retain Andalucian influences, with red-tiled roofs, horseshoe windows and intricate metalwork. Front doors are studded and outside walls painted with whitewash or a luminous blue, which gives a unique sense of lightness. The crafts of Morocco, particularly leatherwork, carpentry and woven cloth, are alive and well throughout the medina.

Chechaouen's old centre is the sloping Place Uta el Hammam, its central fountain surrounded by cafés where *kif* (hashish) is openly smoked, a 15th-century *hammam* (public bath), the Grand Mosque, one of Chechaouen's oldest buildings, the kasbah and, beyond town, twin peaks of the Rif Mountains. A great place at any time of day, the Uta el Hammam comes into its own during prayer time and at night.

The kasbah, which dates back to the 17th century contains a folk museum. Many of the clothes, jewellery and household objects on display are still used in town.

The blue doors and whitewashed walls in Chechaouen keep the evil eye out

2
Essaouira

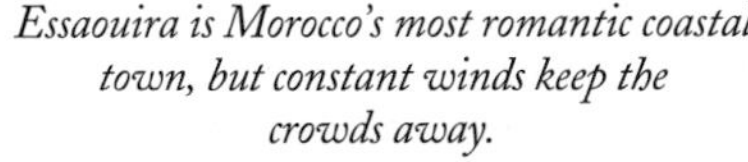

Essaouira is Morocco's most romantic coastal town, but constant winds keep the crowds away.

The isles are what first attracted people to Mogador. The cluster of offshore islands were home to shells from which purple dye, beloved of Roman emperors, was extracted. The islands, now bird sanctuaries, can be visited with a permit (via the tourist office).

Essaouira owes its grand houses and imposing walls to the decision of 18th-century Sultan Sidi Mohammed to create a trading centre. He moved the Jews of Agadir north and had a Frenchman build defences (his work can still be admired at the Porte de la Marine). Linking foreign ships to Saharan caravans, Essaouira was soon handling half of Morocco's foreign trade.

The port is recommended for a stroll at any time of day, but is particularly beautiful at sundown, when catches are landed and hooks baited for the next trawl. Appease your hunger at make-shift fish grills or Chez Sam's restaurant. Trans-Saharan caravans are a thing of the past, but Essaouira still has excellent souks. One of the local specialities are inlaid objects made from thuja wood. Carpenters can be seen at work around the North Bastion. Local rugs and other crafts are displayed in the museum.

Artists have also made their mark on Essaouira. Orson Welles filmed *Othello* here in 1949; Jimi Hendrix came for peace and love in the 1960s. More recently an extraordinary group of local painters and sculptors have attracted an international reputation thanks to the efforts of Frédéric Damgaard, whose gallery is their showplace. These self-taught artists, inspired by tribal traditions, are producing unique, bright and primitive works of art.

29D4

173km north of Agadir

Museum

Derb Laaloui

Wed–Mon 8:30–noon, 2:30–6. Closed Tue

Cheap

Beautiful Essaouira has inspired a colony of artists and skilled craftsmen

Galerie Frédéric Damgaard

Avenue Oqba Ben Nafia

Daily 9–1, 3–7. Summer, daily 8–8

Free

Fish grills at the port (£) Restaurant de la Port (Chez Sam) and Chalet de la Plage, both recommended (££)

Buses to Agadir, Safi, Marrakech and Casablanca

ONCF bus to Marrakech connecting with the train to Casablanca and Rabat

None

Haha coast (➤ 55), Imouzzer-Ida-Outanan (➤ 53)

3
Jbel Toubkal

29D4

Via Imlil (65km from Marrakech)

Basic restaurant and cafés in Asni and Imlil. Restaurant at Hotel de Toubklal, Asni (££)

From Marrakech and Taroudannt to Asni

None

Free

Asni (➤ 79), Imlil (➤ 79), Ouirgane (➤ 79), Marrakech (➤ 74–8), Tin-Mal (➤ 82), Tizi-n-Test (➤ 22–3)

Regular trucks from Asni to Imlil. Information on climbing Jbel Toubkal as well as hiring guides or mules can be had from Club Alpin Français at Imlil

Ramblers and serious mountaineers attempt to climb Jbel Toubkal

The highest mountain in north Africa sits at the centre of a string of Berber villages and a wonderful national park.

On a clear day, the snowcapped peaks of the High Atlas dominate the horizon in both Taroudannt and Marrakech, but Jbel Toubkal, the highest of the peaks at 4,167m, is usually seen only as you climb higher. Imlil is a good starting point for walks in the park and up Toubkal. Guides and mules can be hired by the day. The Toubkal ascent is usually done in 2 days, with a night spent at the Neltner Hut (3207m), run by the Club Alpin Français.

The paths up to Toubkal are very popular. The village of Aroumd is an hour's walk up from Imlil through walnut trees and upland valleys. Two hours further up through goat pastures, a row of houses and kiosks sells refreshments to climbers and pilgrims to the Berber shrine of Sidi Chamharouch. The steep climb to the Neltner Hut takes 2–3 hours. From Imlil, it is also possible to walk east to Tacheddirt and Oukaimeden or west to Ouirgane (both places have hotels). For all these trails, proper walking boots are recommended.

The national park is home to a profusion of birdlife, including larks, dippers, vultures and golden eagles. Berber herders raise Barbary sheep and grow cereals, fruit and vegetables, while the valley sides are often lined with olive, almond, walnut and pomegranate trees. Wildflowers are particularly lush in the spring, becoming smaller, spikier and more hardy as you climb.

4
Jemaa el Fna

Throughout the day and for much of the night, the Jemaa el Fna pulls Marrakechis and tourists into a swirl of activity.

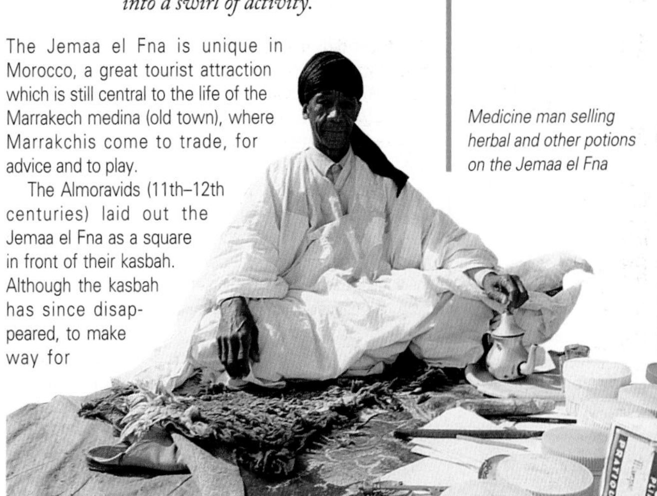

Medicine man selling herbal and other potions on the Jemaa el Fna

The Jemaa el Fna is unique in Morocco, a great tourist attraction which is still central to the life of the Marrakech medina (old town), where Marrakchis come to trade, for advice and to play.

The Almoravids (11th–12th centuries) laid out the Jemaa el Fna as a square in front of their kasbah. Although the kasbah has since disappeared, to make way for the Koutoubia (► 75), and official functions like executions, proclamations and displays moved to the south side of the city, the Jemaa el Fna has kept its audience. It remains the beating heart of the city and is the place to come to see the complex mixture of people who make up the character of this extraordinary city.

The meaning of its name is disputed. 'Place of the dead' is the most common translation, although the place is filled with the living from morning to night. Surrounded by shops, cafés, souks, the post office and Club Med, the tarmac is first ringed by a line of nut, date and orange juice stalls. In the circle that they create, snake-charmers, medicine men with displays of herbs and animal parts, *Gnaoua* musicians, *guerrabs* (water carriers), shoe-shines, story- and fortune-tellers and monkeys perform. During daylight, their audience is mostly foreign. At dusk, rows of food grills set up and, attracted by the smell of sausages, Marrakshis arrive, the elderly in *burnous* and *fes* (tarbouch), the young in jeans and trainers, farmers, bureaucrats and students. In the darkness, the swirling smoke, circles of people, the chants, drum beats and shuffling feet remind you that this is Africa and that until recently, Marrakech had more visitors from the south.

77C2

Marrakech

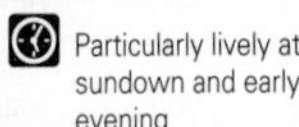

Particularly lively at sundown and early evening

Several cafés (£) and Restaurant Argana (££). The terrace of the Café de France is an excellent viewing platform

Marrakech

None

Free

Souks de Marrakech (► 21), Marrakech (► 74–8)

Be prepared for the attentions of *faux-guides*

5
Médersa Bou Inania

58B2

Talaa Kebira, Fès el Bali

Sat–Thu 9–5. Fri 1–5. Closed at prayer times

Café Nouria in the Bou Jeloud gardens recommended for its calm (£). Lunch at grills near Bab Bou Jeloud (£) or Dar Saada and Dar Tagine palace-restaurants in Fès el Bali (££)

Fès railway station

None

Cheap

Fés (➤ 60–3)

The largest and most costly medersa of Fès is one of Morocco's most exquisite buildings, a perfect marriage of the earthly and the spiritual.

The Merenid dynasty (1248–1554) is responsible for many of Morocco's most accomplished buildings. The artistic high point of the dynasty were the reigns of Sultan Abou Hassan (1331–51) and of his son Abou Inan (1351–8), who deposed him. Abou Inan's medersa was built on what was, at the time, empty land beyond the Qaraouiyne Mosque and was intended to rival the mosque's political and spiritual power.

Médersas were Koran schools where students lived in simple cells off a central courtyard and received both religious and political instruction. Abou Inan's hope, at a time of political instability when there were as many as 2,000 medersa students in Fès, was that these students would feel privileged to live in such a sumptuous building and would remain loyal to him when they left.

Although the prayer hall is still in use, the medersa is open to non-Muslims out of prayer times. From the street, marble steps lead to the central courtyard and a fountain. The decoration is profuse and, in true Andalucian style, is executed in a variety of materials – marble, plaster, carved cedar and zellij tiles. Its proportions are perfect. On either side there are lecture halls behind cedar screens, while the prayer hall, directly opposite, is reached by a ramp over a small stream of the river Fès, part of the intricate network of rivers and channels which made medieval Fès both sanitary and beautiful.

Across the rue Talaa Kebira, there is a row of 13 windows complete with brass bowls and water spouts – the remains of what is generally assumed to have been a 14th-century water clock.

Ritual ablutions must be performed before prayers

6
Souks de Marrakech

Marrakech is no longer supplied by trans-Saharan traders, but its souks still offer a wide range of Moroccan crafts and other goods.

Enter the colourful and exotic world of Marrakech's souks

The grandeur of old Marrakech was paid for with profits from the trade between West Africa and the cities and ports of the north. Most business is now done with Marrakshis and foreign tourists. The best trade is done in the morning, the quiet hours of the early afternoon are only for tourists, while the souks are at their most crowded late in the afternoon.

Coming from the Jemaa el-Fna, an archway leads to the main covered street, rue Souk Smarine, lined with fabrics, clothes and a few shops for visitors, including a couple of serious antique and carpet shops. Opposite the first major left-hand turning is Souk Larzal, the busy wool market and beyond that Souk Btana for sheepskins. A little further, Souk Smarine reaches a junction. To the right is Rahba Kedima, a square where apothecaries will show you chameleons and turtles and then try to sell you kohl, cochineal and henna or perhaps a slice of dried lizard or gazelle horn.

The right-hand fork of Souk Smarine is Souk el Kebir. Not far past the junction, a right turn leads to La Criée Berbère, where slaves were sold until 1912 and where gullible tourists are now sold carpets (there are good ones, but you're unlikely to be sold them). Beware that the 'guides' who tell you that today is the day of the 'Souk Berbère' will often bring you here.

The left hand fork of Souk Smarine leads to Souk el Attarine, full of spices and perfumes. Down this alley, on the right, look for Souk des Babouches (slippers) and on the left the souks of Chouari (carpenters) and Teinturiers, decorated with beautiful dyed wool. The Attarine – and the main souk area – ends at Souk Haddadine, the black-smiths, where you will have to bargain hard to get prices down. If you venture beyond here, you may come across the occasional workshop where goods can often be bought more cheaply.

77C3

Best in the morning and late afternoon. Most shops are closed Fri

Cafés (£) and Restaurant Argana (££) around Jemaa el-Fna. Several palace-restaurants in the medina (£££)

Marrakech railway station

None

Free

Jemaa el-Fna (➤ 19), Marrakech (➤ 74–8)

If you enter the souks with either an official guide or a hustler, be aware that the price of everything you buy will be increased to include a commission for them, often as much as 40 per cent

7
Tizi-n-Test

72C2

Marrakech–Taroudannt: 200km. The Tizi-n-Test pass is approximately 130km from Marrakech, 70km from Taroudannt

Sometimes closed by snow, Jan–Mar

Basic cafés near the pass (£). In Ouirgane, Au Sanglier qui Fume and Residence de la Roseraie (££)

Daily buses between Marrakech and Taroudannt via Tizi-n-Test

None

Jbel Toubkal (► 18), High Atlas sights and drive (► 79, 82–3)

Avoid making the descent from Tizi-n-Test to Taroudannt in the dark

Top right: *donkeys and mules, still the main mode of transport in the Atlas Mountains, wait for their owners to return from the market in Asni*

Right: *experience of mountain roads is useful for negotiating the hairpin bends and blind corners of the Tizi-n-Test*

Tizi-n-Test is a small pass in the High Atlas. The road through it, connecting Marrakech and Taroudannt, is one of Africa's finest drives.

The S501 between Marrakech and Taroudannt (for Agadir) follows an old trading route across the High Atlas. The pass is at 2,093m, where a commemorative plaque certifies that the road through it was laid between 1926 and 1932. Asni, Ouirgane, Talaat-n-Yacoub and Tin-Mal (► 79, 82 and 83) are all worth visiting. Be warned that the road is particularly challenging on the 1,600m descent from the high pass to Taroudannt, twisting and turning, narrow, broken up by water from the mountain and without crash barriers.

The fertile valley between Ouirgane and the high pass, watered by the Nfiss river, is the traditional land of the Goundafas, one of several Berber tribes who struggled for control of the High Atlas in the 19th century. In 1906, the rival Glaoui tribe attacked the Nfiss valley and burned the kasbah of Talaat-n-Yacoub. As a result, the Goundafa built the castle of Agadir-n-Gouf, a few kilometres before Tin-

Mal, in 1907. France, who colonised Morocco in 1912, made political bargains with the Berber rulers: the Glaoui leader was created Pacha of Marrakech, while the Goundafa remained in control of the High Atlas. After capturing Taroudannt in 1913, the Goundafa leader was acknowledged as the effective ruler of the south.

The best views are to be had from the TV relay station a kilometre before the pass, or slightly below the pass. In clear weather there is a magnificent view of the last of the High Atlas villages, the Sous plain and the Anti-Atlas mountains.

8
Vallée du Dadès

73D3

Skoura, the first stop along the Dadès, is 42km east of Ouarzazate

Many cafés (£) and, especially in the gorge, hotel-restaurants (££)

Grands taxis and, in more remote places, lorries are the most likely public transport

None

Free

South sights (➤ 84–90)

Deep gorges, winding roads and Berber kasbahs mark the Dadès river as it cuts its way through the Atlas foothills and heads for Ouarzazate.

The Dadès river flows from the Atlas mountains to the Barrage El-Mansour-Eddabbi, near Ouarzazate, where it joins the Draa river. Most visitors go upstream along what is promoted by some travel companies as the 'Valley of a Thousand Kasbahs'. Skoura, home of the Haskourine tribe, is the first oasis in the harsh landscape, over 40km from Ouarzazate and one of many places to look out for ksour (fortified mud-built settlements large enough to enclose whole villages) and kasbahs (home to single extended families). In Skoura and El-Kalaa M'Gouna, the centre of rose cultivation, thousands of litres of rose essence are exported each year. Skoura stages a rose festival each May.

Beyond Boumalne, the landscape changes as the Dadès runs through a gorge in the Atlas Mountains, a spectacular place which used to be famous for its bandits and lions but is now known for red, volcanic rock, wonderful buildings and trout (good fishing). There are ksour all along the road, but those at Aït Arbi are particularly striking. About 10km further up at Tamnalt, the limestone walls have been worn into fantastic and suggestive shapes. The road is laid with tarmac as far as Aït Oudinar, but becomes increasingly beautiful beyond there.

The Oued Dadès cuts through a harsh and barren landscape, providing water for a few oases along the way

9
Ville Impériale de Meknès

Moulay Ismail's imperial city was one of the world's great palaces, rival to Versailles, but after his death it began a long decline.

Intricate zellig tiling and stucco-work ornament the sanctuary of Moulay Ismail's Mausoleum

Moulay Ismail was governor of Meknès for six years before he became sultan and when Marrakech and Fès objected to his accession, he moved his capital to Meknès. Thousands of slaves built the palace-city, home to Ismail's hundreds of wives, 800 children and infamous negro army. Meknès most famous monument, the excellently-preserved Bab Mansour, constructed of ancient columns from Volubilis, was one of the principal entrances to the imperial city. Appropriately, it leads to the Koubbet el Khiaytin, a small pavilion where foreign ambassadors would be received and, across the road, to the great man's mausoleum. Built while he was still alive, it is a richly ornamented building where Moroccans still come in numbers to pray.

Beyond the mausoleum, an entrance on the left leads to one of Morocco's most unusual sights, the Dar Kebira. Ismail's palace was originally a series of grand buildings. According to Moulay Ismail's chroniclers, when the work was finally completed in 1677, the sultan sacrificed a wolf, whose head hung over the entrance. It is now home to thousands of people who have incorporated surviving ancient walls, arches and vaults in their modern houses.

The scale of Ismail's project can be seen a mile away, beyond Ismail's Dar el Makhzen, part of which is still a royal palace, in the Dar el Ma (the House of Water, also known as Heri es Souani). These were the imperial granaries, large enough to feed the city for years. The rows of arched siloes still maintain their grandeur. The nearby Aguedal basin (400m by 100m), dug to ensure a constant supply of water, is now a popular picnic place. Beyond it lies Heri el Mansour, the ruins of the imperial stables for 12,000 horses.

64C1

Mausoleum: 9–noon, 3–6. Closed Fri.
Koubbet: 9–noon, 3–6.
Dar el Ma: 9–noon, 3–6

Wonderful café at Dar el Ma/Heri es Souani

None

Free (Moulay Ismail's Mausoleum: cheap; Koubbet el Khiaytin: cheap; Dar el Ma: cheap)

Meknès (➤ 63–6)

Heri el Mansour is officially closed to visitors, though entry is sometimes possible

10
Volubilis

- 30B2
- 29km from Meknès
- 8AM–sunset
- Café at the site. Good restaurants (£–££) and bar at nearby Hotel Volubilis (➤ 99)
- Bus and Grands Taxis from Meknès to Moulay Idriss. Private taxi (5km) from Moulay Idriss
- Nearest train: Meknès
- None
- Moderate
- Ville Impériale de Meknès (➤ 25), Meknès (➤ 63–6), Moulay Idriss (➤ 69)
- Antiquities from Volubilis, including beautiful bronze busts, can be seen in the Archaeological Museum, Rabat

The most important archaeological site in Morocco is also the most beautiful, set in rolling farmland beneath Jbel Zerhoun.

Volubilis was one of North Africa's most important cities. Already settled in neolithic times, it entered a golden age when North African-born King Juba II 'of Mauritania' (Roman Morocco) established his capital here in AD 24. Volubilis flourished by trading in olive oil, corn and animals, particularly lions and elephants. Sitting on the empire's southern frontier, it was defended by several hilltop forts, then by a wall with 40 towers. Under Emperor Diocletian (284–305), it was left to Berber tribes, though it remained important until Idriss II (son of the saint buried nearby – ➤ 69) developed Fès. In the 18th century Moulay Ismail used the stone to build his new city of Meknès.

The visit is well marked, leading over the Oued Fertassa to an oil press. The path leads to the paved forum, the arch-walled courthouse (basilica) and the Capitoline temple, dedicated to Jupiter, Juno and Minerva. The Triumphal Arch in honour of Emperor Caracalla and his mother Julia Domna (her image decorates the right-hand medallion) was reconstructed in 1933. Turning right, the grand Decumanus Maximus was lined with shops and colonnades, behind which stand the remains of the largest houses containing beautiful mosaics.

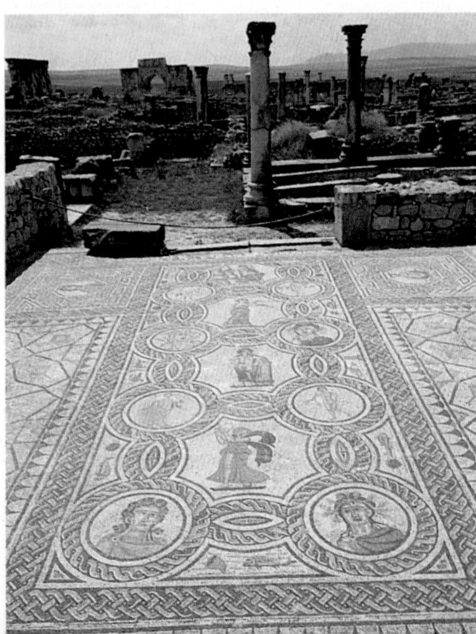

The mosaic at the Cortege of Venus is one of Volubilis' finest

What To See

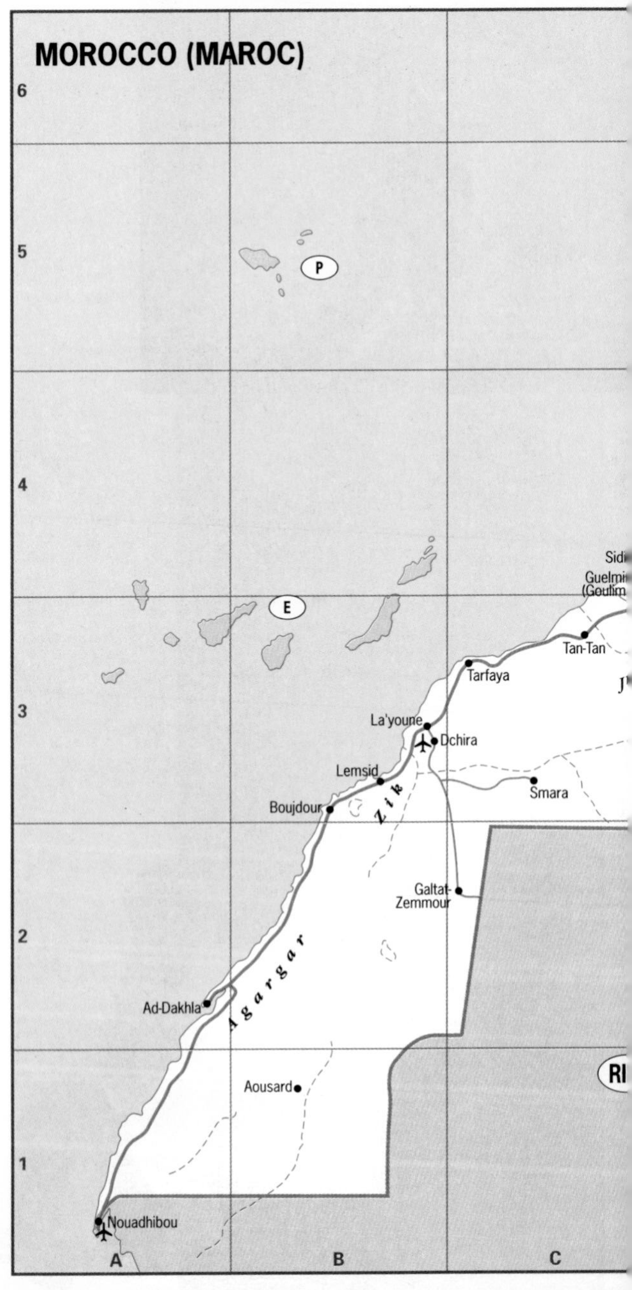
MOROCCO (MAROC)
6
5
P
4
Sidi
Guelmi
(Goulim
E
Tan-Tan
Tarfaya
3
La'youne
Dchira
Lemsid
Smara
Boujdour
Zik
Galtat-
Zemmour
2
Agargar
Ad-Dakhla
RI
Aousard
1
Nouadhibou
A
B
C

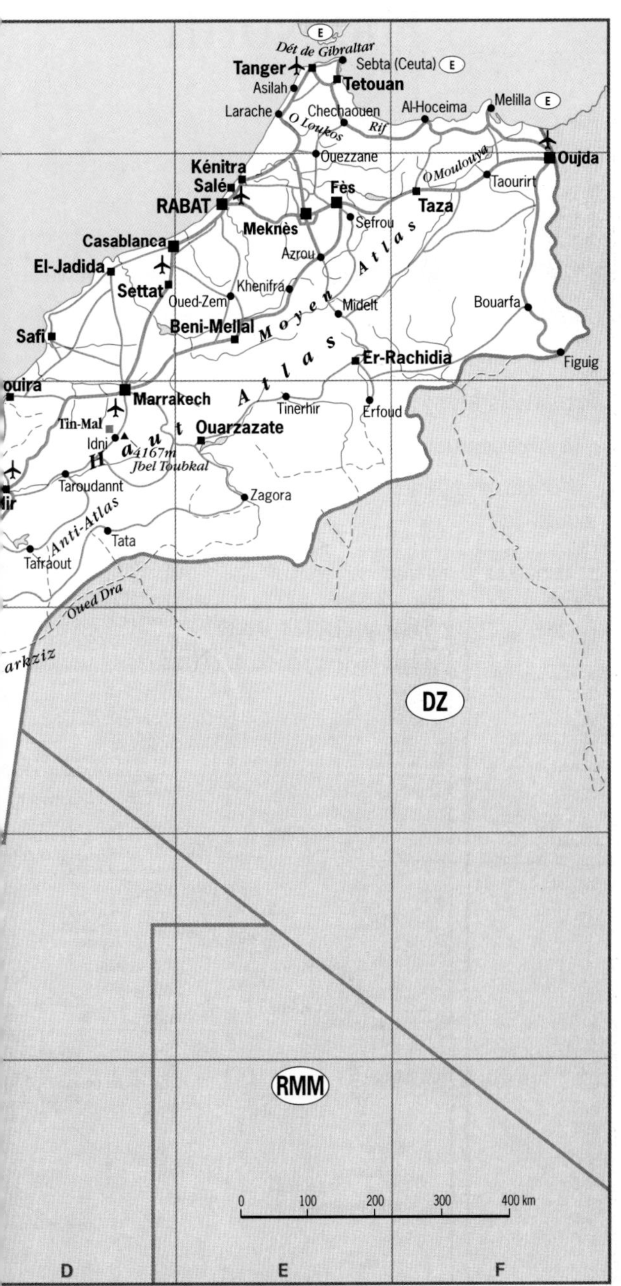
E
Dét de Gibraltar
Tanger
Sebta (Ceuta)
E
Tetouan
Asilah
Larache
Chechaouen
O Loukos
Rif
Al-Hoceima
Melilla
E
Ouezzane
Oujda
Kénitra
O Moulouya
Taourirt
Salé
Fès
RABAT
Taza
Meknès
Sefrou
Casablanca
Azrou
Moyen Atlas
El-Jadida
Settat
Khenifra
Oued-Zem
Midelt
Bouarfa
Beni-Mellal
Safi
Er-Rachidia
Figuig
Marrakech
Haut Atlas
Tinerhir
Erfoud
Tin-Mal
Ouarzazate
Idni
4167m
Jbel Toubkal
Taroudannt
Zagora
Anti-Atlas
Tata
Tafraout
Oued Dra
DZ
RMM
0
100
200
300
400 km
D
E
F

The North

The Rif Mountains acted as a barrier between central Morocco and the Mediterranean world and towns here carry the imprint of the different arrivals from the north. In Tetouan and Chechaouen, founded by Moors fleeing the fall of Seville and Granada, that influence is Andalucian. In Tanger, an open city, it is international. In Al-Hoceima and Larache and the Hispanic colonies of Sebta and Melilla it is Spanish while the Rif coast is now acquiring a new identity as an international resort.

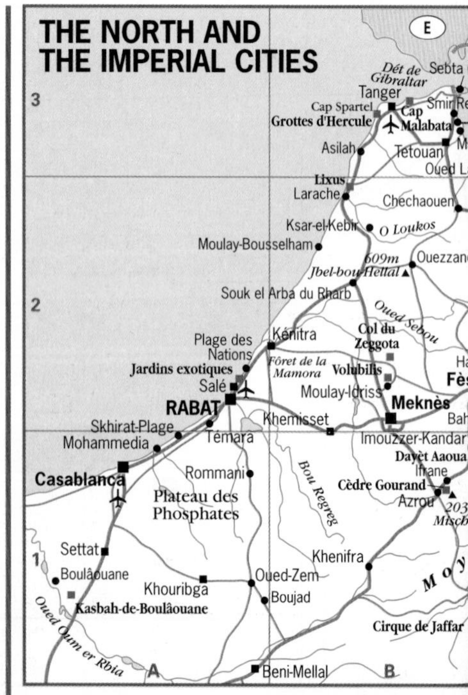

Tribespeople in the Rif Mountains, hardened by the constant threat of invasion, have a fierce reputation which was put to the test as recently as 1924 when 14,000 died in the Spanish retreat from Chechaouen to Tetouan.

'For anybody inclined to be a crook, Tangier offers a setting almost too perfect to be believed, although four different codes of law are in force.'

JOHN GUNTHER
Inside Africa
(Hamish Hamilton, London 1955)

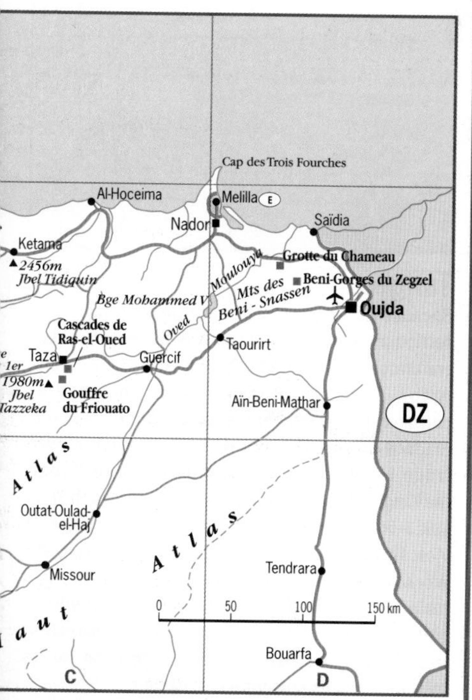

Souvenirs from all over Morocco are on sale in Tanger's souks, but here, as elsewhere, bargaining is a must

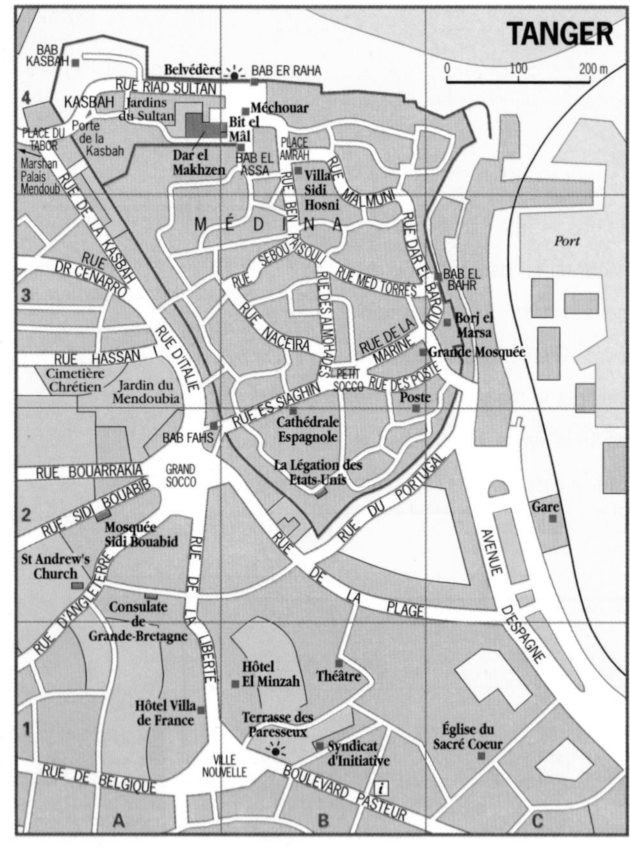

Tanger

Because of its strategic importance, Tanger was settled as early as 750 BC and is Morocco's oldest continuously-inhabited city. Phoenicians, Romans, Arabs, Tunisians, Portuguese, Britons had all controlled Tanger before Sultan Moulay Ismail made it Morocco's main port. The French moved trade to Casablanca and diplomacy to Rabat, leaving Tanger to an international authority (1923–56), when it became a legendary centre of vice. Returned to Morocco since 1956, its migrant workers, foreign residents and plentiful tourists maintain its individuality. It is still an international city, a meeting place of cultures and an inspiration to writers and artists, unique in Morocco for its tolerance and its cosmopolitan flavour.

A Walk Around Old Tanger

Start at the El-Minzah Hotel (➤ 102), walk down rue de la Liberté and take the first alley to the right.

Stairs lead down to a market where women from the countryside sport wide-brimmed pompon hats.

Follow rue de la Plage to the left, towards the Grand Socco (➤ 35). Walk towards the Jardin du Mendoubia (➤ 35), then up steep rue d'Italie which becomes rue de la Kasbah. Turn left at the Kasbah and pass some wonderful Moorish villas. Pass the Marshan stadium to the Forbes Museum (➤ 35). Returning towards the stadium, ask for directions to the nearby Café Hafa (➤ 93). Return towards the medina and at Place du Tabor enter the gate of the Kasbah. Follow rue Riad Sultan to the Méchouar and Dar el Makhzen Museum (➤ 34).

Admire the superb view over the sea from the Belvédère, to the left.

Distance
2km

Time
2 hours without stops, half a day with stops

Start point
El-Minzah Hotel
32B1

End Point
Hotel Continental
32B3

Lunch
Marhaba
67 rue de la Kasbah
937643. Good Moroccan food à la carte or set menus

Continue through the gate towards Place Amrah. Go left down rue Cheikh Mohammed ben Saddik and right where the road splits under the archway. Where the road forks take a right into rue Warcha and at the end left in rue Melouia. Turn around the corner, right into rue Tinsift, right again and then left in rue Torres. At the crossing with rue Dar el Baroud, take a left to Hotel Continental (➤ 102) for a drink on the the great terrace.

The terrace beyond the Bab el Bahr or Sea Gate commands stunning views over the sea and Tanger

If you get lost in the Kasbah, ask to be directed towards the Continental Hotel, which is always near by.

What to See in Tanger City Centre

32A4
place de la Kasbah
932097
Wed–Mon 9–noon, 3–6
Next door Café Detroit (££) for lunch and tea
Tanger Tourist Office, 29 boulevard Pasteur (934151)
None

KASBAH AND DAR EL MAKHZEN ✪✪✪

The kasbah, a citadel since Roman times, forms the highest and most picturesque part of the medina. The British destroyed the old Portuguese fortress in 1685 and what is left today was built by Sultan Moulay Ismaïl in the 17th century. At the turn of the century British eccentrics like Richard Hughes and Walter Harris built sumptuous palaces within the kasbah, still the playground of foreign millionaires. The Méchouar or the place de la Kasbah has two gateways: Bab el Assa, the 'Gate of Watchfulness' leading to the medina and the Bab er Raha, the 'Gate of Winds' leading to a crumbling terrace with views over the straits. The stunning 17th-century Dar el Makhzen was used as a palace in 1912 by Moulay Hafid, his four wives and sixty concubines. Now a museum, it houses a good collection of Moroccan crafts and antiquities found in the northern region and Volubilis (► 26). The palace walls enclose a peaceful and mature Andalucian garden filled with orange and lemon trees and elegant palms.

32B2
8 rue/Zankat d'Amerique
935317
Mon, Wed, Thu 10–1, 3–5 or by appointment. Reference library open for scholars and students
None
Free

LA LÉGATION DES ETATS-UNIS ✪✪

The easiest approach to this quiet museum and beautiful house is from Zankat Portugal, climbing up the steps to the gateway leading to the medina. A few metres to the left is the gate of the oldest American consulate in the world, established in 1821. The ground floor has a permanent art collection of Moroccan and foreign artists who worked in Tanger, while the first floor contains most of its period furniture and a valuable collection of prints and maps.

Riffian women selling their wares – a carpet exhibited at the American Legation

MÉDINA ✪✪

The Petit Socco, once famous for male prostitutes and boy brothels, is now a quiet square with cafés and shops, a good base for exploring the winding alleys of the medina. The rue es Siaghin, leading to the Grand Socco, is the main thoroughfare, lined with souvenir shops and the Spanish Catholic church. To the left, two alleyways lead to the old Jewish quarter or mellah, still containing several synagogues. On the other side of the Petit Socco, rue de la Marine passes the Grande Mosquée (closed for non-Muslims), and a 14th-century medersa (Koranic school).

32B3

PALAIS MENDOUB (FORBES MUSEUM) ✪✪

The old palace of the sultan's representative (mendoub) was restored by American millionaire Malcolm Forbes, who filled part of it with his extensive collection of military miniatures. There are several detailed tableaux of important battles and a strange collection of gifts from Egyptian governors. The gardens are splendid with sweeping views over the sea.

Off map 32A4
rue Shakespeare
933606
Fri–Wed 10–5. Closed Thu
Few
Free

VILLE NOUVELLE ✪✪

The Place de France is the heart of the new town, with excellent café terraces (➤ 92–3) from which to watch the world stroll by. Boulevard Pasteur, now Avenue Mohammed V, is the central artery for a web of streets with restaurants, nightclubs and bars. The square is overlooked by the French consulate. Nearby is the Terrasse des Paresseux, the terrace for the lazy ones, with canons, shoe-shine boys and great views over the straits. The Grand Socco, linking the old and the new towns, has a good market on Thursdays and Sundays. Sultan Mohammed ben Youssef demanded Morocco's independence here in 1947.

32B1

Above: *the alleys off the Petit Socco lead into quieter residential areas worth exploring*

What to See in the North

AL-HOCEIMA ✪

- 31C2
- 325km east of Tanger
- Very crowded in mid-summer, closed in winter
- Café-restaurant Paris (£)
- Buses from Tetouan, Chechaouen, Oujda and Fès
- Al-Hoceima Tourist Office, rue Tarik-ibn-Ziyad (981185/985476)

This relaxed beach town, built by the Spanish in the 1920s, is a good place to stop out of season, before the package tourists arrive. In spite of its airport, Al-Hoceima remains a sleepy beach resort. Its main attraction is a view of the Spanish island of Peñon de Alhucemas with its pretty whitewashed houses. The best beach is 1km west of town in Asfiha.

Note: The beautiful road from Chechaouen to Al-Hoceima should be avoided as it goes via Ketama (see below) and is lined with sometimes very aggressive *kif* dealers.

ASILAH ✪✪

The fishing port is undoubtedly the best part of this busy, well-maintained town on the Atlantic coast. Whitewashed houses and narrow streets, reminiscent of the Greek islands, are enclosed within 16th-century Portuguese walls. The old quarter is accessible through the Bab el-Bahr (Sea Gate) and the Bab Homar (Land Gate). Asilah's main sight is the Palace of Raisuli built in 1906. Caid Raisuli was famous in pre-colonial Morocco as a bandit who became viceroy of the north after kidnapping an American millionaire and the English journalist Walter Harris. The palace, used in August for an International Festival, is closed for the rest of the year. In the southern corner of the town is an interesting cemetery with the *marabout* of Sidi Mansur. The beach is vast and attracts crowds in summer.

At first, Asilah may appear like a Greek island, but soon enough the long Spanish influence becomes apparent

- 30B3
- 46km south of Tanger
- Thu souk
- Chez Pepe (££)
- Regular buses to Tanger, Meknès, Fès, Rabat and Tetouan, trains to Tanger, Rabat, Casablanca
- Few
- Free

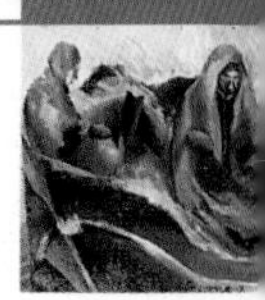

CAP MALABATA ✪

The bay east of Tanger is an uninterrupted curve of appartments and villas, as far as the lighthouse of Cap Malabata, a growing resort with good beaches. Club Mediterranée occupies the grounds of the Villa Harris, now sadly closed to the public. The Times correspondent Walter Harris was famous for his adventures in Morocco and for his homosexual affairs, although his wife finally divorced him on the grounds that he spent too much time gardening. Near the Melaleh estuary are the ruins of a Portuguese fortress, and close to the beautiful Murissat beach stands Château Malabata, a striking turn-of-the-century gothic castle, inhabited by a friendly Moroccan farming family.

- 30B3
- About 10km east of Tanger
- Mar-bel (££), on the beach in Malabata
- Bus 15 from Grand Socco in Tanger or grand taxi
- Few

CAP SPARTEL AND GROTTES D'HERCULE ✪✪

The road to Spartel passes the area known as La Montagne, the Mountain, with many luxurious villas and a few royal palaces. The beaches are beautiful but as this is where the Mediterranean meets the Atlantic Ocean the tides can be very dangerous. Just below the lighthouse are the Caves of Hercules, natural formations enhanced by the erosion caused by the quarrying for millstones.

- 30B3
- 14km west of Tanger
- Daily 9–sunset, best late afternoon
- Drinks on terrace of Miramar (£), lunch at Le Mirage (££) (➤ 92)
- Grand taxi from Grand Socco in Tanger
- Cheap

CHECHAOUEN (➤ 16, TOP TEN)

KETAMA ✪

The small town of Ketama is beautifully set amongst pine woods, at the foot of the often snow-peaked Jbel Tidiquin. This was a popular hill station at the time of the Spanish protectorate, but as the regional centre of the illegal *kif* or hashish trade, it is not without its dangers. The Route de l'Unité, built in the early 1960s by volunteer labour from all over Morocco, goes from Fès to Al-Hoceima via Ketama, and is one of the country's most dramatic roads, but is too dangerous a drive to recommend today.

- 31C2
- 65km from Chechaouen
- Hotel Tidighine (££)
- Daily buses to Fès, Chechaouen and Al-Hoceima

From the lighthouse at Cap Spartel there are startling views over the wild Atlantic beaches

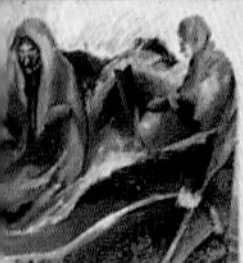

In the Know

If you want to get the real flavour and feel of the country here are some ideas.

10 Ways To Be A Local

Take life easy, don't rush.
Whoever you meet, smile and ask how they are: 'Ca va? Labès?'
Avoid drugs. The police take the law seriously.
Try the foodstalls early evening in Marrakech or Meknès; provided it serves a crowd,you can be sure it is fresh.
Love the king, love Islam, love Morocco.
Sit on a café terrace and make a *café au lait* last a few hours.
Forget about knives and forks and eat with your right hand.
Go to the *hammam* or steam bath for a good rub.
Invite your friends to a multi-course meal and serve them a good couscous.
Be confident in the medina, it is not as difficult as the *faux guides* say.

5 Good Places To Have Lunch

Fish stalls in the harbour of Essaouira (£). Fresh catch grilled while you wait.
Hotel-restaurant de l'Hippocambe (££–£££), Oualidia (☎ 346461). Fresh oysters and seafood served on the terrace with an exceptional view over the laguna.
Buy a picnic at the Marché Central in Marrakech and head for the gardens or mountains for lunch with a view.
Small café-restaurants around Marché Central, Casablanca (particularly good fish).
One of the palace-restaurants in Fès el-Bali.

An open-air food festival offers 1,001 tastes every day at dusk at the Jemaa el Fna, Marrakech

10 Top Activities

Golf: is King Hassan II's passion and there are fourteen excellent golf courses in beautiful

locations. Royal Moroccan Golf Federation ☎ (7)755960 fax: 751026
Swimming: Most towns have a municipal pool and luxury hotels often allow non-residents to use theirs for a fee or if you are having a meal.
Hiking: Endless opportunities for hiking in mountains, forests or countryside. There is a wide network of refuges, guides and hired pack-mules. Royal Moroccan Federation of Skiing and Mountaineering ☎ (2)203798 fax: 474979
Tennis: Most luxury hotels now have tennis courts.
Skiing: Possible during several months of the year with Alpine skiing in Oukaïmeden and winter sports at Mischliffen in the Moyen Atlas.
Fishing: Morocco's coastline is a paradise for anglers, while the lakes and rivers of the Moyen Atlas have trout in abundance (season starts 31 March).
Surfing: Good winds and huge waves make the Atlantic coast ideal for surfers. The best places are Essaouira ('Windy City Africa') and Dar Bouazza near Casablanca.
Hunting: The hunting season is usually from Oct–Mar, with quail, doves, snipe, pheasants, wild boars etc. Moroccan Hunting Federation ☎/fax (7)707835
Horse riding: The horses are usually excellent and the landscapes are amazing, an ideal combination for riding. Royal Moroccan Federation of Riding ☎ (7)754424, fax: 754738
Running: The desert marathon lasts a week and covers 250km over dunes and rocks. Information Cimbaly BP58, 10002 Troyes Cedex. France ☎ (33) 25820128 fax: 25820723

Best Festivals Or Moussems

- Marriage Moussem in Imilchil: last week of September or 1st week of October. Berber Moussem in the Atlas where traditionally marriages are arranged.
- Ramadan: Ninth month of the Islamic calendar. The month of fast is taken seriously in Morocco.
- Ben Aissa Moussem in Meknès: Birthday of the prophet.
- Moussem of Moulay Idriss in Moulay Idriss Zerhoun: September. Largest religious moussem.
- Folk Festival: June. Music and dance, mountain Berbers and desert people in a spectacle in the el Badi Palace, Marrakech.

Cafés With A Good View

- Café Hafa, Tanger (➤ 93). Sweeping views over the Mediterranean.
- Café Maure, Rabat. Views over the medina, the estuary and the sea.
- Café de Paris, place de France, Tanger. Views over Tanger's crowds from morning till evening.
- Café de l'hôtel de Paris, Jemaa el Fna, Marrakech. Excellent views at sunset on the smoky square (➤ 19), the medina and the snowcapped mountains.
- Café in Heri es-Sourani, Meknès. Views over the imperial city and Agdal pool.

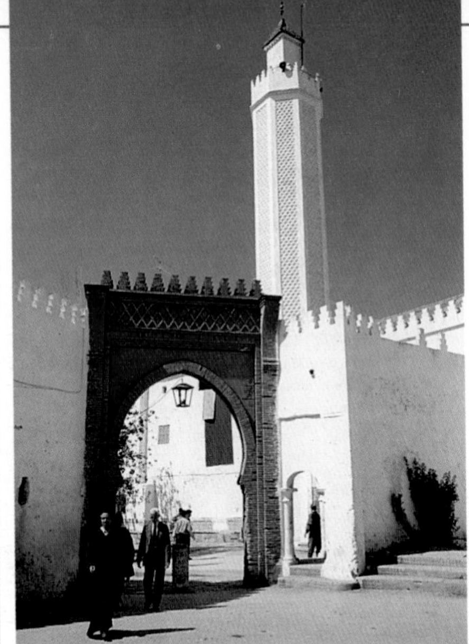

The pleasant town of Larache, with its picturesque medina, is still off the tourist circuit

LARACHE ✪✪

A Spanish protectorate until 1956, Larache is a pleasant town with good paellas and a medina sloping towards the sea. The souks are well stocked, the hassle is minimal and prices are more reasonable than in many cities, perhaps because this is a place where Moroccans come on holiday. Near the lively fishing harbour are the ruins of the 16th-century Kebibat Fortress. The Archaeological Museum, in a 15th-century Portuguese fort at the edge of the medina, contains finds from the Roman city of Lixus which was founded by the Phoenicians. The ruins of Lixus are across the estuary, with an acropolis complex, amphitheatre and a bath house with beautiful mosaics of Neptune.

- 30B2
- 96km south of Tanger
- Museum: Wed–Sun 9–noon, 3–5:30; Lixus: daily by daylight
- Café-restaurants (£)
- Bus 4 to beach and Lixus, or boat across estuary
- Tourist information, avenue Mohammed V (914454)
- Few
- Museum: cheap; Lixus: free

MELILLA ✪

Melilla has been a Spanish enclave since 1497 and does not feel Moroccan at all. The old quarter of Medina Sidonia, enclosed by 16th-century walls, shows an interesting mixture of Spanish and Moroccan architectural styles, but otherwise there is little excitement. This is not a place to linger, unless you are interested in the duty-free shops. The Museo Municipal has a small collection of Roman pottery, coins and maps.

- 31D2
- Northeast coast, 120km from the Algerian border
- Museum: Tue–Thu, Sat–Sun 9–1, 4–6
- Metropol (£) Plaza España
- Several ferry services to Málaga and Almería in Spain, buses to Nador
- Museum: cheap

MOULAY-BOUSSELHAM ✪✪

This small resort, named after a 10th-century Egyptian saint, has a fantastic but dangerous beach. The lagoon of Merja Zerja is safer, but is most famous as a paradise for flamingos and birdwatchers. Nearby Souk el-Arba du Gharb comes to life during the Wednesday market.

- 30B2
- 140km south of Tanger
- Hotel le Lagon (£)
- Casablanca-Fès/Tanger line

OUEZZANE

The lovely market town of Ouezzane, founded in the 18th century by a religious teacher, soon became an important religious centre. The medina has some of the most interesting architecture in the Rif, with cobbled streets, tiled roofs and a green-tiled zaouia with an octagonal minaret. Place de l'Indépendence is the centre, usually packed on Thursdays, day of the souk. Ouezzane is famous for its excellent olive oil and its woollen carpets sold in the weavers' souk or the Centre Artisanale (place de l'Indépendence).

- 30B2
- 60km southwest of Chechaouen
- Café-restaurants on the main square (£)
- Buses to Chechaouen, Fès and Mèknes

Women displaying the handmade rugs for which Ouezzane is famous

OUJDA

Oujda, on the Algerian border, has little to offer the traveller but is the perfect base for exploring the stunning Beni-Snassen mountains with the Zegzel Gorge and the hot water spring of the Cave of the Camel. The souk is authentic and relaxed, including the Souk el-Ma where water was sold to irrigate the gardens. The main gate into the medina is the Bab Sidi Abd el-Ouahab, above which the heads of villains were hung on poles. The small Lalla Aisha gardens are refreshing, and contain a small ethnographic museum (9–noon, 2:30–5:30). Six kilometres from the medina, boulevard Sidi Yahia leads to the supposed tomb of St John the Baptist, revered by Jews, Christians and Muslims.

- 31D2
- On the Algerian border
- La Chaumière (££)
- Buses to the main cities
- Trains to Tanger, Fès, Meknès, Rabat and Casablanca

RIF COAST

The long beach strip between Sebta and Tetouan is in full touristic development. New resorts at Smir Restinga, Mdiq and Cabo Negro have several large hotels with all water-sport facilities. Martil with its 18th-century kasbah is the favourite summer resort for Tetouanis, but east of the more relaxed Oued Laou, the cliff coast is often frequented by hashish smugglers. When tourist numbers increase sufficiently and direct flights from Europe become more regular, the Rif coast is likely to experience something of a building boom.

- 30B3

SEBTA (CEUTA) ✪✪

- 30B3
- 38km northeast of Tanger
- Fish restaurants by port
- Buses to Tanger, Casablanca, Al-Hoceima, and Nador.
- Tourist Office, Muelle Cañonero Dato, by the port (509275)

A Spanish enclave since 1580, there is little of interest apart from the duty-free shops. Border crossings are slow. Within the ramparts is the Plaza de Africa with two baroque churches and opposite the port is a small archaeological museum (Tue–Sun 9–1, 5–7). Above the old town towers Monte Acho with good views across the sea. The mountains of Gibraltar and Ceuta, forming the shortest crossing to Africa, have been known as the Pillars of Hercules since ancient times.

TETOUAN ✪✪✪

- 30B3
- 57km east of Tanger
- Musée Archéologique: Wed–Mon 9–noon, 2–6. Musée d'Art Marocain: Mon–Fri 8:30–noon, 2:30–5:30, Sat 8:30–noon
- (➤ 93)
- Buses to Fnideq, Tanger, Chechaouen, Meknès and Fès, and to the beaches on the Rif Coast
- Tourist Office, 30 rue Mohamed V (961915)
- None
- Both museums cheap

Above: *everyday life in the busy alleys of Tetouan's medina*

Famed as the 'daughter of Granada', Tetouan remains a beautiful and fascinating city to explore. Founded in the 15th century by Muslims who had fled Granada and become rich working as corsairs in the port of Martil. When it became the capital of the Spanish protectorate in 1913, the Spanish built an elegant new town outside the walls. Place Hassan II, dominated by the glittering Royal Palace, is the heart of the city. In the corner, Bab er-Rouah leads into the medina which may need a guide to explore. The main drag through the souk is rue Terrafin, leading to Bab el-Okla and the Musée d'Art Marocain which has a collection of local costumes, crafts and musical instruments, set in an Andalucian garden. Left of rue Terrafin is the Souk el-Houts with pottery and fish and the Guersa el-Kebir, the textile souk. Also off place Hassan II is the entrance to the mellah and boulevard el-Jazaer, home to the Musée Archéologique, with it's small collection of Phoenician, Roman and Muslim finds. (See Lixus ➤ 40).

A Drive South of Tanger

Leaving Tanger you have a choice of taking the Asilah/Larache road, or making a detour by heading for the northwest tip of Africa at Cap Spartel (14km) (➤ 37) and the Caves of Hercules and ruins of Roman Cotta.

From here the beautiful beach stretches 45km to Asilah, but strong currents makes it unwise to swim.

Beyond Asilah (➤ 36), the road cuts inland, passing Souk Tnine and the junction for Tetouan before returning to the ocean at the site of Roman Lixus and, 4km further, the pleasant resort of Larache (96km from Tanger) (➤ 40). Beyond Larache the road leaves the ocean again.

Follow the Oued Loukos through some of the lushest farmland in Morocco and pass the site of the battle of the Three Kings (1578), which ended with the death of the Portuguese king and Portuguese ambitions in the area.

The main road bypasses Ksar (36km from Larache), as do most visitors unless it's Sunday (souk day).

Distance
175km (without side-trips)

Time
A pleasant day out, *en route* to Meknès/Fès or Rabat

Start point
Tanger
30B3

End point
Souk el Arba du Gharb
30B2

Lunch
Café Central ✉ place de la Libération, Larache (£–££).

Bab el Khemis, Larache

Arbaoua, the next town, marked the frontier between French- and Spanish-controlled Morocco. There is also a turn-off for the popular resort of Moulay-Bousselham and the Merja Zerja lagoon with its spectacular wildlife (➤ 40).

South of Arbaoua, a town has built up around the next major junction (Souk el Arba du Gharb), near the ruins of Roman Banasa. From Souk el Arba, you can either head southeast towards Meknès and Fès, or southwest along the P2 to Kenitra and Rabat.

Atlantic Coast

You could happily spend your entire trip to Morocco along the Atlantic coast, exploring some of the country's oldest settlements, its capital (Rabat) and commercial centre (Casablanca), some beautiful towns, including Essaouira, and some wonderful landscape, particularly along the Haha coast.

Agadir, the country's main beach resort, has little to do with Morocco. There are other places for a beach holiday – Oualidia, for instance – but you'll have to hunt for discos or international fast food chains (though they are spreading). The region also produces two of Morocco's outstanding crafts: blue-and-white pottery from Safi and thuya wood objects from Essaouira.

These coastal towns and cities tend to have a very different feel to interior Morocco, perhaps because many were held by Europeans or were international ports.

'Morocco is like a tree nourished by roots deep in the soil of Africa which breathes through foliage rustling to the winds of Europe.'

KING HASSAN II
of Morocco, *Le Défi*, translated by Anthony Rhodes as *The Challenge* (1979)

Rabat

Rabat became Morocco's capital under French colonial rule and is now one of the country's most cosmopolitan cities. As the political centre it houses embassies and government buildings along the broad avenues of the *ville nouvelle*. But the ramparts, the kasbah, the medina and the Tour Hassan are a reminder of the city's long history.

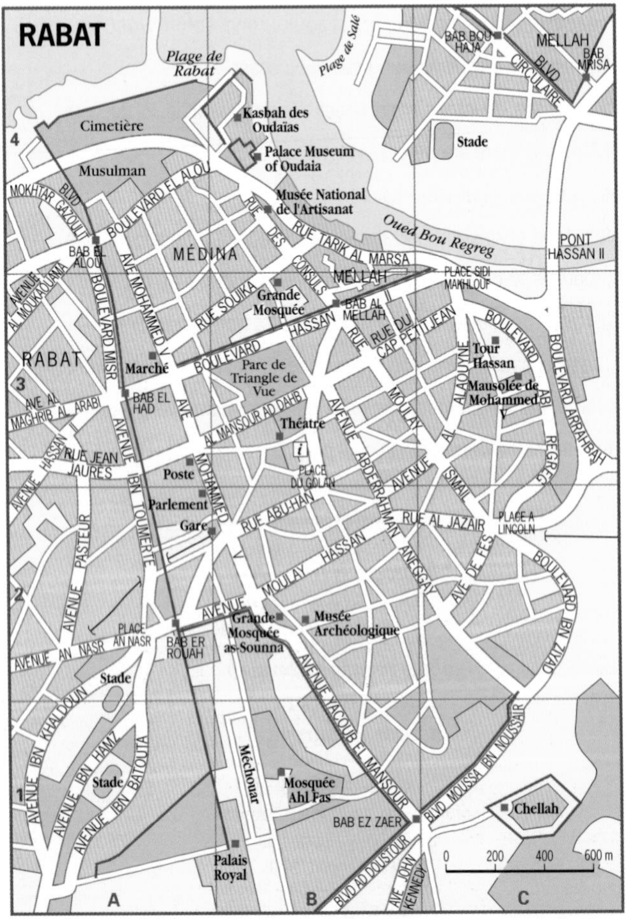

Spectacular gateway to the lush and overgrown necropolis of Chellah

What to See in Rabat

CHELLAH ✪✪

This walled necropolis of the Merenid sultans was built between 1310–1334, more or less over the ruins of ancient Sala Colonia. This enchanting site is entered by a gate flanked by two semi-octagonal towers. The stairway descends into lush gardens with the remnants of the Roman site and a sacred pool where black eels eat eggs fed to them by barren women hoping for fertility. Further on are the Merenid buildings (mosque and zaouia) and the tombs, of which the most impressive are the tombs of Abu Hassan and of his wife Shams ed-Douna, decorated with verses describing her amazing funeral.

46C1
Near Bab ez Zaer
8:30–sunset
None
Rabat Tourist Office, 22 avenue d'Alger (730562) and rue Patrice Lumumba
Cheap

KASBAH DES OUDAÏAS ✪✪✪

Originally a *ribat*, it was settled by the Andalucians and then later by the rebellious Oudaia tribe who set up camp in it. The 12th-century gateway is a marvel of Moorish architecture. (Ignore the unofficial guides who hang out near by who will tell you that the kasbah is closed for prayer time. It is not.) The 12th-century Kasbah Mosque on the main street is the oldest in town. Rue Bazzo leads to the Museum of Moroccan Arts, housed in a 17th-century palace where the great Moulay Ismail once lived. Attached is a peaceful Andalucian garden. The interior is worth seeing as much as the interesting collection of arms, jewels, carpets and musical instruments.

46B4
Kasbah des Oudaïas
731537
Wed–Mon 8:30–noon, 3–6. Closed Tue. Kasbah always open
Café Maure (£)
None
Cheap

46A4
Most shops closed Fri afternoon
Street stalls with food (£)
Few
Free

MÉDINA ✪✪

Unlike medinas elsewhere in Morocco, the medina of Rabat is small, uncomplicated and a safe place to wander around. Most of the architecture dates from the 17th century when Andalucian Muslims built a wall within the vast Almohad ramparts, known as the Andalucian wall (see also walk ➤ 49).

46B2
23 rue Brihi, near the Chellah Hotel
701919
Daily 9–noon, 2:30–5:30. Closed Tue
None
Few
Cheap

MUSÉE ARCHÉOLOGIQUE ✪✪

A good collection of artefacts from Sala Colonia and some of the exceptional Roman bronze statues from Volubilis (➤ 26).

RAMPARTS ✪✪

Rabat's 5km-long Almohad walls enclose not only the medina and the kasbah but also the palace and the new town. The Bab er Rouah, the gate of winds, is the most remarkable of its five gates. Contemporary with the Kasbah gate (➤ 47), it is elegantly decorated with arabesques and Koranic verses in Kufi script. The upper rooms are occasionally opened for temporary art exhibitions. The Royal Palace was built during the 18th century within the southeastern corner of the ramparts, but mostly rebuilt by the present king who added a private golf course.

Above: *neither money nor effort was spared on the richly decorated Mausoleum of King Mohammed V*

46C3
Near place Sidi Makouf
Open daily; Mausoleum daily 8–6:30
None
Few
Free

TOUR HASSAN ✪✪✪

The unfinished 45m-high minaret of the Hassan Mosque stands out on Rabat's skyline. The grand building was abandoned the day Yacoub el-Mansour died (1199) and a lot of the materials were used for other buildings. The minaret would have been 64m high (80m with the lantern). Each face is finely decorated with different stone-carved geometric designs. Nearby is the Mausoleum of Mohammed V, the first king of independent Morocco and father of the present king. His white marble tomb is richly decorated with typical Moroccan motives.

A Walk in the Medina of Rabat

Start at the Bab el Had, where an opening in the walls leads to a vegetable market. Beyond the market, take a left turn on to avenue Mohammed V, then turn immediately right to reach rue Souika.

At the intersection with rue Sidi Fatah stands the 19th-century mosque of Sultan Moulay Sliman. Further along the same street is the grand mosque of the Merenids, entirely rebuilt in the 19th century. The only survivor of the Merenid mosque is the 14th-century fountain opposite the mosque.

Further on, rue Souika turns into covered Souk es-Sebat.

Here the products of some of Morocco's best craftsmen were once sold, though today there is little of temptation. A reconstructed arch at the end of the souk leads into rue des Consuls, so called because in the 18th and 19th century European consuls and merchants were obliged to live here. The street has some wonderful old foundouqs: follow your nose and take a look around. The grandest is No 109, the Foundouq ben Aicha. At the end of the street, opposite the kasbah is the Souk el-Ghezel, once the wool market for the carpet weavers, now filled with wood carvers and joiners.

Shopkeeper at Rabat's medina

Cross the road towards the splendid Bab Oudaïa and enter the kasbah (► 47). Walk along the main street (rue Jemaa) to the oldest mosque in Rabat, the 12th-century Jamaa el-Atiq, and a platform with amazing views over the estuary and the river. Return on the same street and take a left down rue Bazzo to the museum (► 47).

Distance
1.5km

Time
3 to 4 hours with stops

Start point
Bab el-Had
46A3

End point
Palace Museum of Oudaïa
46B4

Lunch
Grill cafés around the vegetable market near Bab el-Had (£). Café Maure (£) (► 39)

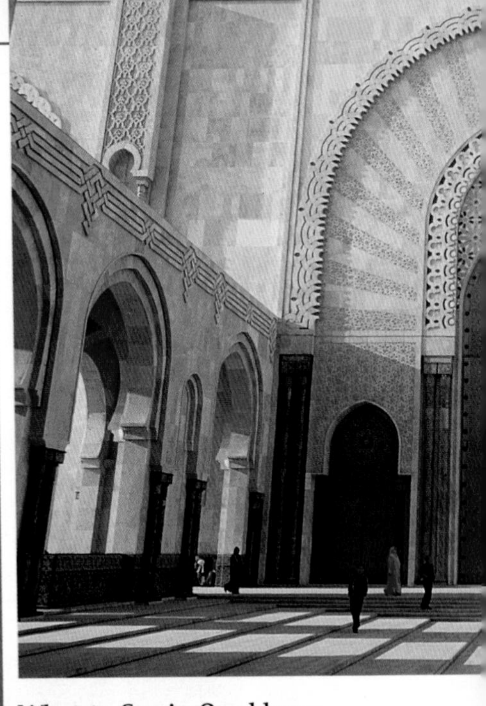

What to See in Casablanca

72C4
Casablanca Tourist Office, 55 rue Omar Slaoui (☎ 271177) and 98 boulevard Mohammed V (☎ 221524)

Forget the legendary film with Humphrey Bogart and Ingrid Bergman, entirely shot in Hollywood: Casablanca has few historical monuments. But as the country's economical and industrial capital, and main port, it does have a character all of its own.

At first sight it appears a modern city with high-rise office buildings and elegantly dressed people along its avenues, but the problems of industrial development and population growth soon become apparent: homeless street kids, sprawling *bidonvilles* or slums and an enormous gap between rich and poor. This isn't an obvious place for tourists, but it does have one of the most hassle-free souks in the country.

72C4

AIN DIAB ✪✪

Casablanca's coastal resort is lined with clubs, restaurants and bars popular with Moroccans and Arabs, who come to enjoy the pleasures denied them in their own country, including women and alcohol. A new Saudi Palace with library and mosque overlooks the beach.

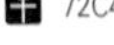

72C4

ANCIENNE MÉDINA 

Casablanca's old medina dates from the end of the 18th century and has few old buildings or craftsmen at work. The easiest entrance is from place Mohammed V. Most shops sell Western-style clothes and bric-à-brac.

In fulfilment of the Koranic verse 'The throne of God was built on water', Hassan II built his mosque on land that had been reclaimed from the Atlantic Ocean

GRANDE MOSQUÉE DE HASSAN II ✪✪✪

The 200m-high minaret dominates Casablanca's skyline, while the 22-acre prayer hall beneath it is three times the size of St Paul's Cathedral in London. The interior is lavishly decorated with marble and carved stone, cedarwood cupolas and gilded ceilings which slide open to let the sun in. This is King Hassan II's most extravagant building project; its cost, put at £500million, is said to have been met entirely by public subscription.

- 72C4
- On the Corniche
- 442315
- Sat–Thu guided visits, check by phone as times vary. At other times, entry for Muslims only
- Good
- Very expensive

NOUVELLE MEDINA (QUARTIER HABOUS) ✪✪

A French interpretation of a medina, built in the 1930s, the Habous district is a nicer place to stroll than the old medina and a more likely place to look for crafts or antiques. The olive market is a marvel while the Balilda vegetable and spice market has many herbalists and fortune tellers.

- 72C4
- boulevard Victor Hugo
- Closed Fri afternoon
- Café terrace at the centre (£)
- Bus 5 from boulevard de Paris

SIDI ABDERRAHMANE ✪✪

The marabout on the tiny islet, west of the city centre, contains the tomb of Sidi Abderrahmane from Bagdad. It is believed to have miraculous healing powers.

- 72C4

VILLE NOUVELLE ✪✪

The centre of the new town is the place Mohammed V (place des Nations Unis) with elegant 1920s colonial buildings. The musical fountain doesn't always work, but the Parc de la Ligue Arabe is a shady place. The covered Central Market has excellent café grills at lunch time.

- 72C4

A tour of El-Jadida's ramparts and streets, with their European flavour, makes for a pleasant stroll

What to See on the Atlantic Coast

AGADIR ✪

72B2
Jun–Sep, Mon–Fri 8–3; Oct–May, Mon–Fri 8–noon, 2:30–6:30
Agadir Tourist Office Immeuble A, place Prince Héritier Sidi Mohammed (846377); boulevard Mohammed V (840307)

Vallée des Oiseaux
boulevard de 20 Août
Daily 9:30–12:30, 2:30–6:30

Bert Flint Museum
avenue Mohammed V
840784
Mon–Sat 9:30–1, 2:30–6

Agadir, meaning 'fortified granary', has acquired a bad reputation as an overcrowded, cheap package-tourism resort with a large number of hotels, good and bad, but then it has a vast beach and a wonderful climate which allows swimming most of the year round. The reason for Agadir's proliferation of hotel's is the 1960 earthquake, which destroyed most of the old town. What has been built isn't so bad, but the rest of Morocco is both more beautiful and more exciting. The ruined 16th-century kasbah with panoramic view is the city's only reminder of its historical importance. Below the kasbah lies the port where fresh sardines can be sampled from one of the café-grills.

The **Vallée des Oiseaux** is a pleasant garden with bird cages and a little zoo. A visit to the **Bert Flint Museum**, with its wonderful collection of southern Moroccan handicrafts is a must if you're heading south.

AZEMMOUR ✪✪

72C4
117km south of Casablanca
Grill-cafés at the entrance of the medina (£)
Train from Casa, Rabat, Fès, Meknès and Tanger, buses to El-Jadida, Casablanca, Marrakech

This striking town, its white medina built on a cliff along the river, has been a trading post for centuries. A rampart walk is a good way to explore the Portuguese walls, while a tour of the medina reveals more Portuguese influence. In the Kasbah, which functioned as the Mellah or Jewish

Traditional handmade shoes, baskets, sweets, amber or herbs: you want it? you get it

quarter, climb the tower of Dar Baroud for a panoramic view. Haouzia, just outside town, is a pretty beach.

EL-JADIDA ✪✪

The 16th-century medina was on an island until the Portuguese did some landfill. They held it for 250 years. The old Cistern in its centre (Mon–Fri 8–noon, 2–6 cheap), has an amazing subterranean vaulted interior. The coast north of El-Jadida is one long beach, but Sidi Bouzid to the south is both cleaner and more fashionable.

- 72C4
- 100km south of Casablanca
- Chikitos (£)
- Buses to Safi, Marrakech and Casablanca
- Trains to Casa, Rabat, Tanger, Fès and Meknès
- Tourist Office, avenue Ibn Khaldoun (344788)

Orson Welles made part of his film Othello *in the atmospheric subterranean cistern at El-Jadida*

ESSAOUIRA (► 17, TOP TEN)

IMOUZZER-IDA-OUTANAN ✪✪

A refreshing day trip from Agadir, or the perfect place for a picnic though you will not be alone on weekends. The long winding road into the hills passes the aptly named Vallée du Paradis, where the river cuts through straight cliff faces and palm trees provide more than enough shade. Immouzer is a lovely village at the foot of the High Atlas, with an excellent hotel and a good souk (Thursdays). Paths from the Hotel des Cascades (► 96) lead after 4km to the waterfalls, only spectacular after the winter. Locals will dive from the rocks for a few dirhams.

- 72B2
- 61km northeast of Agadir
- Waterfall in the spring
- Cafeterias near the waterfall (£), excellent lunch at Hotel des Cascades with view over the valley (££)
- 1 bus daily from Agadir, behind hotel Sindbad next to the bus station (3½ hours)

JARDINS EXOTIQUES DE SIDI BOUKNADEL ✪✪

A French engineer and botanist created several gardens, marked by colour-coded paths, in the 1950's with Morocco's indigenous plants and others he collected from around the world. Delightful as they are, the gardens are not very well kept and women are sometimes hassled.

- 30A2
- 12km northeast of Rabat
- Daily 9–6:30
- None
- Bus 28 or grand taxi
- Cheap

OUALIDIA ✪✪

With a series of rocky islets creating a lagoon in the ocean, this is one of the calmest beaches on this part of the Atlantic. The beach is vast (particularly at low tide), there is little development and many oyster banks. In short, Oualidia is a simple but idyllic little paradise. In summer it gets very crowded with Marrakechi families.

- 72B4
- 175km south of Casablanca
- Le Parc à huîtres (£)
- Buses to Safi, El-Jadida
- Trains to Casablanca, Rabat, Marrakech, Safi

SAFI

✪✪

72B4
Trattoria Chez l'Italienne (£–££)
Trains to Casablanca and Marrakech via Benguerir; buses to Agadir, Casablanca, Marrakech and Essaouira
Tourist Office rue Imam Malek (622496)

Safi is more an industrial than a touristic town, with a big harbour for the export of phosphates and an important sardine industry. Morocco's sardine catch, mostly landed here and at Agadir, is the world's largest. There are a few Portuguese monuments worth stopping for if you're passing, including the 16th-century Kasr el-Bahr, overlooking the sea (opposite place Sidi Boudhab daily 8–noon, 2–5 cheap) and the old chapel in the medina. The Bab Chaaba area in the souk is famous for the blue-and-white Safi pottery.

SALÉ

✪✪✪

30A2
Across the estuary in Rabat
Cheap restaurants along rue Kechachin
Bus 6 or 12 from avenue Hassan II in Rabat, grand taxis or a little boat from the quay below the kasbah. Note that the petits taxis are not allowed to go across the bridge to Salé

Up until the late–17th century Salé, renowned as a centre of religious learning, was a more important city than Rabat. Coming from Rabat the imposing 13th-century Bab Mrisa, the harbour gate, leads into the medina which is easy to explore, while the smaller gate beside it leads into the mellah or Jewish area. The 14th-century Abul Hassan Medersa in the souk (daily 8–noon, 2:30–6) is the most important building in Salé, intricately decorated with carved wood, *zellij* and stucco. Several foundouqs have survived in the souk area which is more traditional than in Rabat. Every year on the afternoon of the Prophet's birthday there is a procession around the medina when candles are carried on poles and many of the Salé men dress up as pirates, a colourful reminder of the city's past.

TARHAZOUT

72B2
19km north of Agadir
Swimming all year round
Taoui-Fik on the beach behind the camp site (£) and other beach restaurants (£)
Bus 12 or 14 from place Salaam, Agadir
None
Free

Superb and vast beach just north of Agadir with surprisingly little development. A favourite winter hang-out for modern-day hippies, the place is very easy-going.

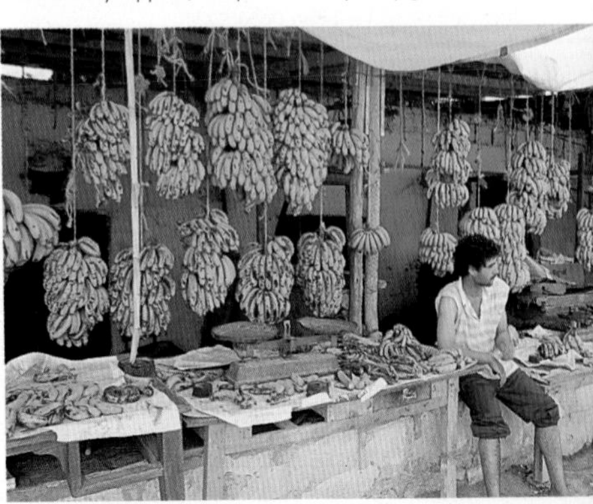

No shortage of bananas on the road out of Agadir, as Banana Valley is only a few kilometres away

A Drive from Agadir to Essaouira

Leave Agadir northwards on the P8.

After 13km, at Tamrhakht, the road is lined with stalls selling bananas from nearby 'Banana Valley'.

Three kilometres further to the left is the campsite of Tarhazout (➤ 54) and a great beach.

Past Tarhazout village there are a few more exposed beaches, but the coastline is already becoming more dramatic as the High Atlas mountains meet the Atlantic. Twenty kilometres further, the lighthouse of Cape Rhir marks the borderline between two important Berber territories, the Ida-Outanan and the Haha.

After 10km the road follows an estuary inland to Tamri, surrounded by banana plantations.

The landscape suddenly changes again after 20km as the road runs through a rich agricultural valley. After another 18km, a left turn leads after 20km to Pointe Imessouane, a remote Berber fishing village popular with surfers.

Return to the P8, which is now lined with arghan trees, and continue towards the regional centre of Tamanar, after 23km. At the signpost to the right for Souk et-Tnine Imi-n-Tlit, 20km further, a dirt track climbs to Jbel Amsittene. Take a right at the first turning and left at the second to reach, after 16km, the 905m-high summit.

From here there are great views over the Haha coast and the High Atlas.

Back on the P8 after a few kilometres the minarets of the small town of Smimou appear. Forty kilometres further north, follow signs left to Sidi Kaouiki.

This is one of the world's great windsurfing beaches, with a small hotel and the shrine of Sidi Kaouiki who is believed to cure infertility.

Return to the P8 and follow it to beautiful Essaouira.

Goats savouring the delights of the bitter arghan trees

Distance
175km on the P8, 252km with turn offs to Pointe Imessouane and Jbel Amsitten

Time
3 hours without stops

Start point
Agadir
72B2

End point
Essaouira
72B3

Lunch
Taoui-Fik (£) good fish restaurant, salads and omelettes ✉ Tarhazout beach (near camping); Berber Auberge (£) ✉ Pointe Imessouane

Moyen Atlas

The heartland of Morocco, blessed with fertile soil, protected from the Mediterranean by the Rif Mountains and from the Sahara by the Atlas, was the obvious place to locate a capital. The Romans built Morocco's most important ancient city at Volubilis. When Sultan Moulay Idriss wanted to build a new capital for his Arab state he didn't travel far. While Fès remains Arab at heart, its nearby rival Meknès is a Berber city. Much of Morocco's history is tied up in these three cities and no visit to the country is complete without them.

The Moyen Atlas might lack the stunning grandeur of the High Atlas, but they make up for it with cedar forests, mountain lakes and waterfalls. You can ski in winter, hunt in autumn and trek in summer. Visit in the spring and the whole landscape will be flower-filled.

'Of all the cities I have seen,
only Constantinople,
viewed across the Golden
Horn from Pera, and
Jerusalem from the Mount of
Olives, compared with Fez
from its encircling hills.'

WILFRED THESIGER
The Life of My Choice
(London 1987)

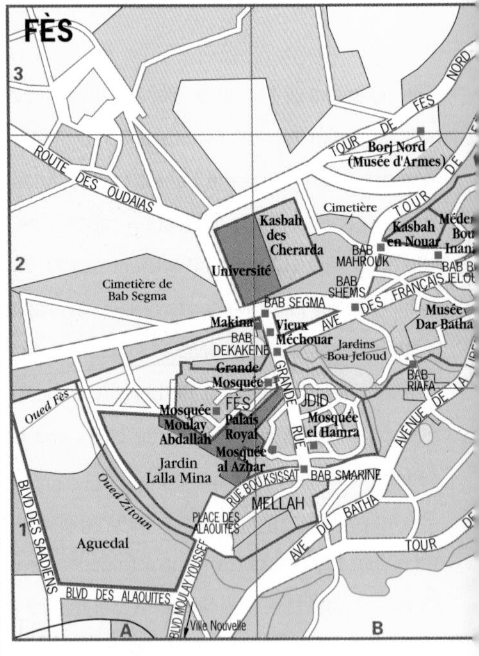

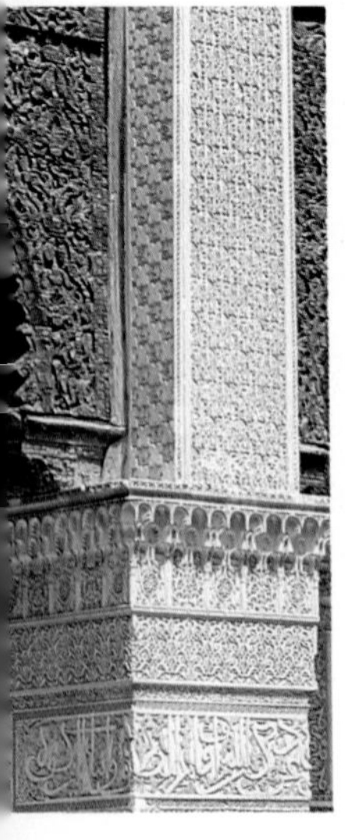

Superb stucco work in the peaceful courtyard of the Médersa Attarine, Fès el Bali

Fès

Mysterious, magnificent Fès, the most complete medieval medina in the Arab world, has world-famous monuments, thousands of winding streets and hundreds of palaces and grand houses. No wonder its people (Fassis) tend to feel a sense of cultural superiority. No wonder, too, that UNESCO has declared it part of the World Heritage.

In AD 789, Idriss I began to create the nucleus of a new Islamic city which was then developed into the stunning capital by his son Idriss II. Fès was Morocco's power-centre until the 16th century, when the capital moved to Marrakech. For 400 years, Fès vied with Meknès and Marrakech to be the centre of Moroccan power, though it always claimed cultural superiority. In 1912, the French built the *ville nouvelle* and moved power to Rabat and Casablanca, leaving Fès el Bali gloriously unscathed by colonial development.

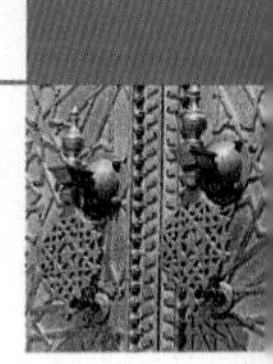

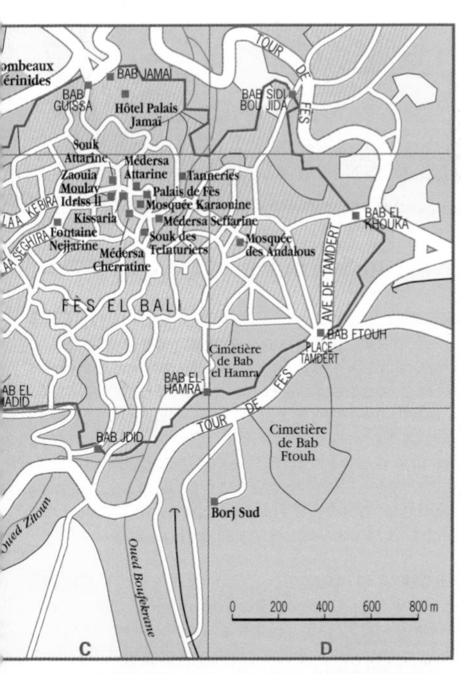

A magical spectacle of shadow and light, the rooftops of Fès' medina at sunset

What to See in Fès

58B1
Excellent Cafe Nouria in Bou Jeloud Gardens (£). Cafés (£) in the Mellah
1, 3, 10, 19, all from Place des Alaouites, opposite palace gates
Fés Tourist Office, place de la Résistance (623460/626279)
Free

FÈS JDID

The Merenids gave Fès her greatest glory and some fine monuments (Medersa Bou Inania, for instance), but Fassis were always suspicious of their southern Berber rulers. As a result, the Merenid sultans built Fès Jdid ('new Fès') outside the walls of Fès el Bali. The site is dominated by the royal palace (closed to visitors). The old Jewish quarter – the *mellah* – Bab Smarine and Bab Dekakène, the Vieux Méchouar where the French quartered their prostitutes and quiet Moulay Abdallah are all worth visiting.

59C2
Fès el Bali
9–noon, 2–6. Closed Fri AM
Nearby café and good restaurants (£–££)

MÉDERSA ATTARINE

Like the later Médersa Bou Inania (► 64), the Attarine medersa (1323–5) is one of Fès's most beautiful monuments. Beyond the great bronze doors, 60 upper rooms were built to house students of Karaouiyine university. The courtyard is an assemblage of exquisite decoration, complicated but wonderfully light. From the roof there are wonderful views of the Karaouine mosque.

59C2
Fès el Bali
Closed to non-Muslims
Nearby café (£), Dar Saada (££)

MOSQUÉE KARAOUINE

Closed to non-Muslims, this is the centre-piece of Fès, large enough for 20,000 worshippers. Built in 859, it is the city's principal mosque and, like Kairouan in Tunis and Cairo's Al Azhar, is a great theological centre. Glimpses of the elaborate interior can be had from its doorways.

58B2
Place L'Istiqlal
634116
8:30–noon, 2:30–6. Closed Tue
Café Noria (£), Bouayad (£)
1, 9, 10, 12, 18
Cheap

MUSÉE DAR BATHA

A palace started by Sultan Moulay Hassan in the late 1800s, the Dar Batha houses the museum of Moroccan Arts. The palace's public rooms are home to a jumble of artistic and scientific objects, illuminated Korans, embroideries, inlaid weapons and blue-and-white Fassi pottery. The exquisite minbar from the al-Andalous mosque, has been on loan since 1992. The central garden, with magnificent trees, is the most compelling attraction.

Left: *ritual ablutions in the magnificent courtyard of the Karaouine Mosque*
Below: *the tanneries*

SOUKS DE FÈS 

Fès prides itself on a tradition of skilled craftsmen. The Talaa Kebira and parallel Talaa Seghira run from near Bab Bou Jeloud to the Mosquée Karaouine. Being the main tourist access, many shops are overpriced. Around the mosque are the Attarine (grocery and spices), Seffarine (brassmakers) and Nejjarine (carpenters) souks. The main pleasure is the discoveries made in little kiosks after you have got lost, never to be discovered again.

59C2
Fès el Bali
8:30–noon, 3–8. Closed Fri
Several cafés (£)
1, 10, 12 to Bab Bou Jeloud. 3, 12, 18 to Bab Ftouh. 10 to Bab Guissa

TANNERIES

The stinking tanneries, on the banks of the Oued Fès must have inspired a few visions of hell. Here animal skins are stripped, cured and dyed in a series of vats. Best visited early or mid-morning, when the dyes are being used.

59C2
Along Oued Fès
Morning visits recommended
Free, though a 'donation' may be requested

TOMBEAUX MERENIDES

The Merenids presided over the glory days of Fès and their tombs attracted the praise of earlier travellers. Only a few walls remain. Beautiful ruins, perhaps, but the main reason for coming here is the view over the city and to visit the nearby Weaponry Museum in the 16th-century Borg Nord.

59C3
Near Hotel des Merinides
Borj Nord: 8:30–noon, 2:30–6. Closed Tue
Café and restaurant (£–££)
Tombs: free. Borj Nord: cheap

ZAOUIA MOULAY IDRISS 

If the Mosquée Karaouiyine is the heart of Fès then this is its soul, the resting place of the city's founder (you can see his tomb through the door, though you may not enter). A place of reverence for all Fassis, it is also a place of refuge for people in search of *baraka* (blessing).

59C2
Fès el Bali
Closed to non-Muslims
Restaurant/café (££)
None
Free

Did you know ?

At the height of its power, in the late 13th century, Fès el Bali was home to 125,000 people (2,000 were students at medersas while 20,000 were weavers). They prayed in the medina's 785 mosques, ate bread from 135 bakers and washed in one of 93 public baths.

A Tour of the Walls of Fès

Distance
15km

Time
1 hour without stops. All day with stops.

Start/end point
Avenue Hassan II

Lunch
Excellent restaurant at Hotel Palais Jamaï ☎ 634331, near Bab Jamaï/Bab Guissa ☎ 635090 (££)

Leave palm-lined Avenue Hassan II towards Fès Jdid. At the fork, take the main Taza-Oujda road down into the Zitoun valley.

The walls of the Mellah of Fès Jdid (► 60) appear on the left and then pull back. As they close in again, Bab Jdid gives access to the heart of the medina. On the right is the ruined 16th-century Borj Sud. Between the next gate (Bab el Hamra) and Bab Ftouh is the cemetery of Mosquée el Karaouine, studded with tombs of holy men. A kilometre past Bab Ftouh, the potteries (look for kiln smoke) are a good place to look for Fassi blue-and-white pottery.

Leave the Taza road as it pulls away from the city and turn left towards Bab el Khouka. At the fork, turn right to avoid entering the city, then left at the next juntion to avoid leaving it completely.

Across the river the road passes a centre of the skin trade (animal, that is).

At the next major junction, turn left towards Bab Jamaï and the Palais Jamaï Hotel.

Beyond the adjacent Bab Guissa (good access to the medina), the road passes a cemetery with excellent city views. For a more dramatic view of all Fès el Bali, turn right to the Merenid Tombs and Borg Nord (► 61).

Many restaurants in the medina offer traditional music to accompany the famous Fassi cuisine

Follow the walls, past the kasbah, and through Bab Segma with its 14th-century tower.

The long wall on the left encloses the palace.

At the next major crossroads, turn left (Boulevard des Saadiens) along more wall, over the railway to reach Avenue Hassan II.

Meknès

In the 17th century, Sultan Moulay Ismaïl chose Meknès, founded in the 10th century by the Meknassas Berber tribe, to build his imperial capital. During his reign (1672– 1727), Meknès achieved the peak of its glory, as it replaced Fès as the imperial capital. Before Moulay Ismaïl's arrival Meknès was a sleepy trading post, while soon after his death his successors moved the capital back to Fès and Marrakech; an earthquake in 1755 destroyed much of his creation. The colonial French had an important army base in Meknès and built their *ville nouvelle* outside the medina and the imperial city. Nowadays Meknès is a lively provincial town, in many ways overshadowed by Fès. It is the centre of the Moroccan wine trade and is famous for fine iron-and-silver work.

30B2

Meknès Tourist Information, place Administrative ben Al (524426) and Esplanade de la Foire (52019)

Free

Bab Mansour is decorated with Roman columns from Volubilis, and was one of the original entrances to the 17th-century imperial city

What to See in Meknès

BAB MANSOUR EL-ALEUJ

Famed as the finest gateway in North Africa, the monumental Bab Mansour has become the symbol of Meknès and was named after its architect. Bab Mansour was completed by the son of Moulay Ismaïl, Moulay Abdellah, who is praised in the inscription at the top. Its twin flanking arcades are supported by marble columns from Volubilis.

64B2

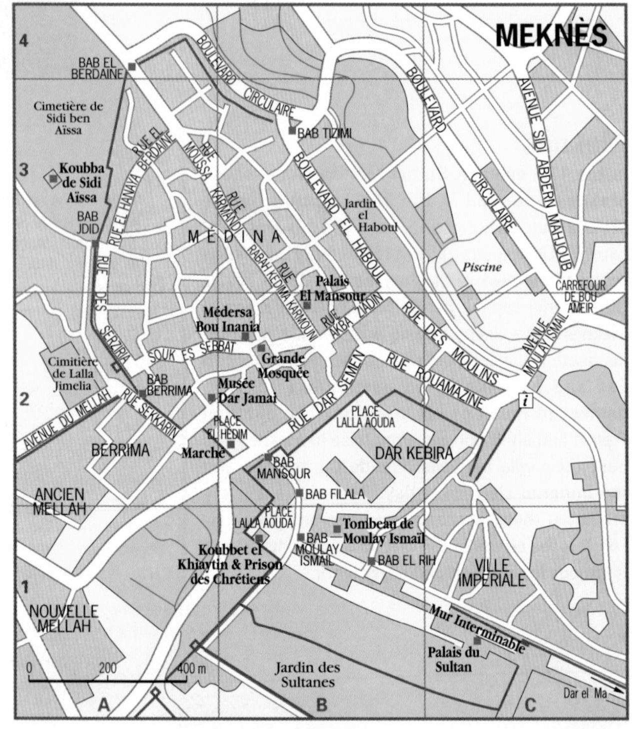

64B2
Souk es Sebbat
Daily 9–noon, 3–6
None
Cheap

MÉDERSA BOU INANIA

This 14th-century Koranic school in the heart of the medina, built around the same time as the medersa in Fès, is one of Morocco's finest. The peaceful courtyard is lavishly decorated with colourful *zellig* tiling, fine stucco and Koranic inscriptions carved in wood. Behind a wooden screen are 40 spartan cells for students, which were occupied until 1964. Stairs lead from the gallery to the roof, from where there is a perfect view over the medina and its mosques, particularly the Grand Mosque.

64B3

MÉDINA

Less mysterious than the souks of Fès or Marrakech, this is one of the easiest medinas to explore without a guide and without hassle. The main street is Souk es Sebbat with clothes, babouches and kaftans. Beyond the Médersa Bou Inania and the Grand Mosque are workshops where iron is inlaid with beaten silver thread, a speciality of the city. Further on is the Palais el Mansour now occupied by a carpet shop but worth a visit for its rich interior. Near Bab el-Jedid, the Koubba of Sidi Aïssa is the tomb of a saint whose followers enter a trance to eat live snakes.

A Walk from the Old Medina

Avoid lunch hour (noon–3) for this walk, as the sites will be closed and even in winter the sun can be strong.

Start at the medina gate, near Jardin el Haboul, which leads to rue Akba Ziadin. About 20m further, turn right into rue Rabah Kedima Karmouni, then left into the Kissaria which leads to the Grand Mosque and the medina's main thoroughfare, Souk es-Sebat.

A further 20m on is the Médersa Bou Inania (► 64).

Continue along the main street for 50m.

Beyond the little mosque, turn left into the street leading to place el-Hédim and Dar Jamai Museum (► 66). Stop for a drink, or walk towards the right of the square to the food market (► 66). Across the square, Bab Mansour (► 63) marks the entrance to the Imperial City (► 25).

Continue to place Lalla Aouda with Koubbet el-Khiaytin (right) and the Royal Golf Club.

Walk through Bab Moulay Ismaïl and find the Mausoleum of Moulay Ismaïl to the left and on through the Bab er-Rih, the gate of the winds. To the left is the Dar Kebira and ahead lies the 1km-long 'Interminable Wall', so-called because prisoners were walked along it to their execution.

Turn right at the end of the wall to reach the wonderful café at Heri es-Souani.

Distance
2km

Time
3–4 hours

Start point
Gate near Jardin Haboul
64B3

End point
Heri es-Souani
Off map 64C1 (Petits taxis back)

Drinks
Terrace on place el-Hédim (£) or café above Heri es-Souani (£)

Meknès is famous for its iron work inlaid with beaten silver thread

The old city of Meknès, built on a plateau, is protected by kilometres of crenellated ramparts

PLACE EL HEDIM ✪✪✪

64B2

Dar Jamai Museum
place el Hedim
530863
Wed–Mon 9–1, 3–6:30. Closed Tue
Cheap

The recently paved 'Square of Destruction' is the best place to start exploring the old city of Meknès or to finish your tour and watch the crowds who come here towards sunset. The Bab Mansour (➤ 63) stands on one end of the square; the Dar Jamai Museum at the other end is worth a visit. Built by the same family as the Palais Jamai in Fès (➤ 60), this 19th-century palace with a peaceful Andalucian garden houses an interesting collection of Moroccan arts. Just off the square to the left is a covered food market with some of the best displays of dates, nuts, spices and olives in Morocco.

RAMPARTS ✪✪

64B2

Moulay Ismaïl surrounded his capital with some 25km of triple walls, to stop both horsemen and foot soldiers. These massive fortifications incorporated some magnificent gates, including Bab Mansour (➤ 63), Bab Berdaine or Gate of the Saddlemakers and Bab el-Khemis which lead to the former *mellah* (Jewish quarter). An inscription on a pediment of the latter gate reads, 'I am a gate which is open to all races, whether from the West or the East'. Near the 12th-century Almohad Bab Jedid there is a small junk market.

VILLE IMPÉRIALE (➤ 25, TOP TEN)

What to See in the Moyen Atlas

AZROU ✪

30B1
77km from Fès, 67km south of Meknès
Hotels/restaurants (£–££)
Buses from Casablanca, Meknès, Midelt, Ifrane, Fès, Khenifra, Marrakech

A small Berber market town with a ruined kasbah built by Moulay Ismaïl, Azrou is an excellent base for hiking in the surrounding woodlands. It is also known for Berber carpets. A good place to check is the Ensemble Artisanal off avenue Mohammed V, or the Tuesday souk.

BENI-MELLAL 

73D4
194km northeast of Marrakech
Restaurant (£)
Buses to Fès, Marrakech, Azilal

A pleasant stop between Marrakech and Fès with an important souk on Tuesday. The Kasbah Bel Kush was built by Moulay Ismaïl but completely restored in the 19th century. Below the Borj Ras el-Aïn are peaceful gardens with a pleasant cafe. Ask for 'La Source'.

CASCADES D'OUZOUD

An interesting excursion from Beni-Mellal, becoming increasingly popular with Moroccan students who camp here in summer. The remarkable waterfalls, 110m high, are one of Morocco's most beautiful natural sites. Avoid crowds at weekends.

- 73D3
- 50km south of Beni-Mellal, 38km from Azilal
- Several cafés (£)
- Buses to Azilal from Marrakech and Beni-Mellal, then grands taxis

IFRANE

The king has a palace here and the town is full of luxurious villas and chalets. There are good walks in the surrounding cedar woods and skiing in nearby Mischliffen. The *dayets* (crater lakes) of Aaoua, Afourgan and Ifrah are popular.

- 73E4
- 17km from Azrou
- Restaurant (£–££). Excellent bakery-patisserie Le Croustillant (£)
- Buses to Azrou, Fès
- Tourist Office, place du Syndicat (566821)
- Skiing Jan–Mar

Morocco's most impressive waterfalls are a popular excursion for local families

IMILCHIL

- 73D3
- Cafés (£)
- By 4-wheel drive, rough roads from Midelt or Khénifra or organised tours
- 2nd or 3rd week of Sep. Wedding festival, check with tourist office in Fès

Tourists usually only venture to this little village lost in the Atlas Mountains in September, when the Wedding festival takes place. Young people from the region come here, all dressed up, in the hope of finding the partner of their dreams. If they do, they get engaged and come back the following year to get married. The festival has become so popular that another one is held for tourists.

IMOUZZER-KANDAR

- 30B1
- 45km south of Fès
- Hotel des Truites (£–££)
- Buses from Fès
- Apple Festival in July, Mon souk

This hilltop settlement, with its two bathing lakes and shady green areas, is a popular escape from Fès. The lively Monday souk is held in the crumbling Kasbah of the Aït-Seghrouchen. The public swimming pool is filled with spring water. North of town, the oasis around Aïn Chifa also has a pool of fresh spring water. A track leads eastwards to the summit of Jbel Abad in the Massif du Kandar, with stunning views over the Saïss Valley and mountains.

KHENIFRA

- 30B1
- 160km from Fès, 129km north of Beni-Mellal
- Restaurant (££)
- Grands taxis from Fès, Meknès and Beni-Mellal

Often called the 'Red Town' because its houses are all painted in the red colour of the soil, Khenifra has two souks (Sundays and Wednesdays) and a reputation as a centre for prostitution.

MIDELT

- 30B1
- 193km south from Fès
- Restaurant de Fès (£)
- Buses to Er-Rachidia, Meknès and Fès

A refreshing stop in summer. The Sunday market attracts Berbers from the surrounding villages. Carpets in this region are excellent and can be bought from the Atelier de Tissage, run by Franciscan nuns in the Kasbah Miriem on the road to Tattiouine. The wild landscapes of the Cirque de Jaffar are only accessible by four-wheel drive.

The lively and picturesque Moulay Idriss with its whitewashed mosques and mausoleums on a hilltop rises like a mirage out of the rural landscape

MOULAY-IDRISS ✪

Moulay Idriss, a descendant of the Prophet Mohammed and founder of the first Muslim kingdom in Morocco in the 8th century, is buried here. The saint is much venerated and five pilgrimages to his tomb were considered the equivalent of one to Mecca. His festival in September attracts huge crowds and is attended by the king. The mosque and tomb are strictly forbidden to non-Muslims, who are also forbidden to stay the night (hence the absence of hotels), but the holy town is an interesting, picturesque place to wander around *en route* to Volubilis.

30B2

SEFROU ✪✪

A market town on the old Saharan trade route, Sefrou was where Moulay Idriss II lived while he planned his new capital of Fès. The medina is one of the country's most beautiful. Its distinctive character is perhaps due to a large Jewish community (no more). Its main claim to fame is now a Cherry festival held in June.

30B2
28km southeast of Fès
Restaurant in the Hôtel Sidi Lahcen Lyoussi (££)
Buses from Fès, Midelt, Er-Rachidia
Tourist Office, boulevard Hassan II (660380)

TAZA ✪✪

Because of its strategical importance in the Taza Gap, controlling the pass between the Rif and Middle Atlas, Taza, which became the Almohad capital in 1141, has a rather bloody history. The old town is dramatically perched on a rock, so a tour of the Almohads walls and gates is recommended. The elegant Méchouar remains the focal point of the Medina and the souks stretch between the 12th-century Grand Mosque and the Andalucian Mosque. Just off the square is the Merenid Médersa of Abul Hassan.

31C2
120km east of Fès
Restaurant (£–££)
Buses to Oujda, Fès, Nador and Al-Hoceima
Trains to Oujda, Fès, Meknès
Tourist office, 56 avenue Mohammed V

VOLUBILIS (➤ 26, TOP TEN)

High Atlas & The South

Many of the images that seduce us into visiting Morocco, and that stay with us after we return home, come from this region. From the epic proportions of the High Atlas and the splendour of Marrakech to the beauty of the desert and the strangeness of the people who live in or near it, with their ksour and kasbahs, palm groves and camels, this region is beguiling. It is also the most difficult to travel through, either because the infrastructure doesn't yet exist or because rain or sand has blocked it. That, of course, is part of its allure: the High Atlas and the South are places which challenge the body and soothe the mind. This perhaps explains why reformist movements have traditionally started in this region. The High Atlas remains the heartland of traditional Morocco. Change comes more slowly here and when it does, the people tend to resist (although they have taken television antennas to their hearts). Spend some time in this region and you'll have more of an adventure than a holiday.

'... the south means not only the Atlas with its feudal chiefs and their wild clansmen, but all that lies beyond of heat and savagery ...'

EDITH WHARTON
In Morocco (1929)

Marrakech

Marrakech is where the African and the Arab have most successfully mixed. Marrakech is grand and yet not without its sleaze, exciting, yet with plenty of places to seek refuge (including perhaps the best hotel in Africa). If you had to choose just one place to visit in Morocco it should be here where you can spend days looking at historical remains, wandering among the best souks in the country, making day-trips to the High Atlas, whose snow-capped peaks hang over the city, or just indulging in some of Morocco's best hotels and restaurants.

rat-Plage
Khemisset
Imouzzer-Kandar
Sefrou
Dayèt Aaoua
mmani
Bou Regreg
Cèdre Gourand
Ifrane
Azrou
▲2036m Mischliffen
Moyen Atlas
eau des sphates
Outat-Oulad-el-Haj
Khenifra
Missour
Khouribga
Oued-Zem
Boujad
Midelt
Cirque de Jaffar
Beni-Mellal
Atlas
ades zoud
Bin el Ouidane
Imilchil
Rich
Gorges du Ziz
Bge Hassan-Addakhil
Azilal
Haut
Er-Rachidia
Boudenib
4071m Igbil M'Goun
Gorges du Dadès
Gorges du Todra
Source Bleue de Meski
Goulmima
Tafilalt
Mgoun
Tinerhir
Erfoud
Sijilmassa
Rissani
El-Kelaa-Mgouna
Boumalne-Dadès
Moulay-Ali-Chérif
O Dadès
Oulad Abdelhalim
Erg Chebbi
Merzouga
Barrage El-Mansour-Eddahbi
Oued Rheris
Oued Ziz
rzazate
Taouz
Agdz
Vallée du Dra
Oued Dra
Zagora
Tamgrout
Amazraou
el Bani
Mhamid
DZ
0 50 100 150 200 km
D E F

Harsh competition between the many juice stalls keeps prices down

The striking decoration of the Dar Si Saïd Museum

What to See in Marrakech

DAR SI SAÏD ✪✪

77C2
East of rue Zitoun el-Jdid
442464
Wed–Mon 9–noon, 2:30–6:30
Cheap
place Abd el-Moumen ben Ali (436239)

This delightful palace houses an impressive collection of Moroccan Arts. The star exhibit is a decorated marble basin from the Ben Youssef medersa. Equally impressive are the collection of Berber jewellery and weapons and the 16th-century wood-carvings from el-Badi.

EL BADI ✪

77C1
Bab Berrima
Daily 8:30–noon, 2:30–6.
Cheap
Marrakech Folk Festival in Jun

The great Saadian King Ahmed el-Mansour built this palace in 1603 and called it El Badi, 'the Incomparable.' The most splendid building in Africa, it fell into ruins soon after his death. Moulay Ismaïl later looted its treasures for his own palace in Meknès (➤ 25). Little is left today, but the vast courtyard, the red *pisé* walls and the sunken gardens are impressive.

JARDIN MAJORELLE (BOU SAF-SAF) ✪✪

76B4
Off avenue Yacoub el-Mansour, Guéliz
Winter, 8–noon, 2–5; summer, 8–noon, 3–7
Few
Moderate

The sub-tropical garden, created in the 1920s by the French Orientalist painter Jacques Majorelle (1886–1962), has been splendidly restored. Shady bamboo groves, lily-covered pools and superb palms make it a most pleasant place to be on a hot afternoon. The walls are painted electric blue which wonderfully offsets the greenery and flowers. The artist's studio is a small Museum of Islamic Arts with Saint Laurent's fine collection of North African carpets and furniture and Majorelle's paintings.

JEMAA EL FNA (➤ 19, TOP TEN)

KOUBBA EL BARAOUDIYN ✪✪

77C3
South of Mosquée Ben Youssef
9–noon, 2:30–6:30
Moderate

This small ablution pavillion is all that survives from glorious 12th-century Almoravid Marrakech. A simple building from the outside, its decoration inside the dome is exquisite and extremely interesting, being the earliest known example of the so-called 'Spanish-Moorish style', later so commonly used all over North Africa and Andalucia.

MAISON TISKIWIN

Hidden behind a wooden port… home to the stunning collec… anthropologist, with jewellery,… from the North and Moyen … knock; one of the assistants m…

MÉDERSA BEN YOUSSEF

Built in the 16th century as… country, this was home for students who studied at the nearby Mosque of Ben Youssef. Go up to the cells the students used to share. In contrast to those small and sparse rooms, the spacious and richly decorated open courtyard appears even more of a jewel. The plan may be simple but the decoration of *zellig* mosaic, stucco and cedar carving never stops to please with its harmony.

Ben Youssef
8:30–noon, 2:30–6:30
Moderate

Elegant stucco calligraphy in the courtyard of the Ben Youssef Medersa

MOSQUÉE KOUTOUBIA ✪✪

The elegant 65m-high minaret of the Almohad 'Booksellers' mosque' dominates Marrakech's skyline and has become even more prominent since the French designed the road system around it. This is the model for all Moroccan minarets with the domed minaret built in the 1:5 proportion to the tower. The three golden balls, surmounted by a tear on the top, are said to be a gift of Sultan Yacoub el-Mansour's wife who melted down her jewellery as an act of penance. Her crime? She had eaten three grapes during the fasting month of Ramadan.

76B2
avenue Mohammed V
Closed to non-Muslims

PALAIS EL BAHIA ✪✪

This lavish palace of a black slave, who rose to become grand vizier, was built in 1880 and later inhabited by the French General Lyautey. It was looted after the vizier's death, but the surviving quarters and the lovely garden with fruit trees give a clear idea of its former grandeur.

77C2
Follow signposts from rue Zitoun el-Jdid
8:30–noon, 2:30–6. Compulsory guided tour
Moderate

Another day, another fabric, and another colour in the Dyers' souk

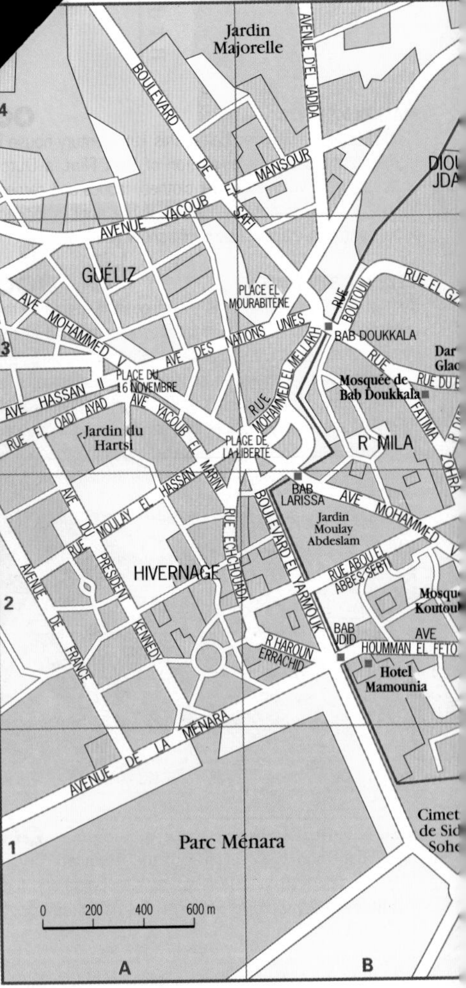

77D3

RAMPARTS ✪✪

A tour of the city walls by calèche is a must. About 16km long with 20 gates and 200 towers, the ride never fails to impress. Most of the walls date from the Almohad period except for the section around the Agdal gardens, which were built under the Almoravids. Several of the gates date from the Almoravid reconstruction of Marrakech's fortifications. The extraordinary Bab Aguenaou is the only surviving Almohad original. From the top of the Bab Dabbagh there is a good view over the tanneries.

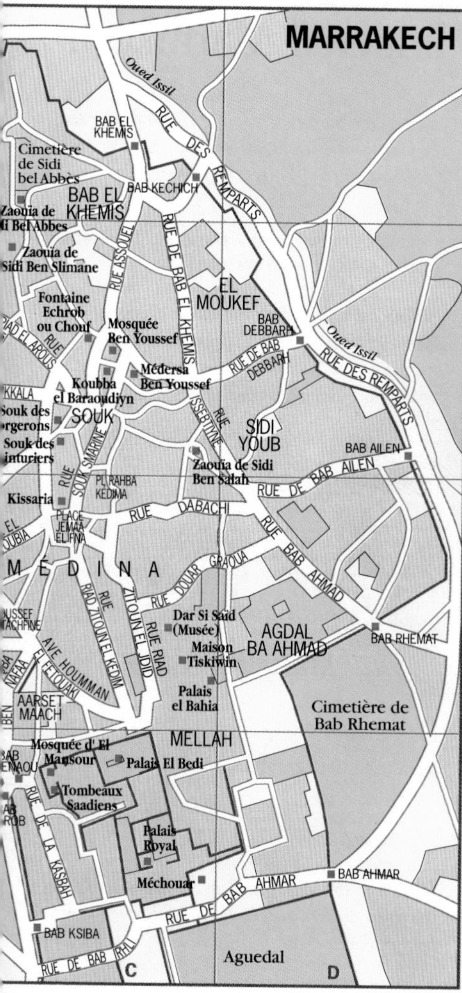

MARRAKECH

Oued Issil
RUE DES REMPARTS
BAB EL KHEMIS
Cimetière de Sidi bel Abbès
BAB EL KHEMIS
BAB KECHICH
Zaouïa de Sidi Bel Abbes
Zaouïa de Sidi Ben Slimane
RUE ASSOUEL
RUE DE BAB EL KHEMIS
EL MOUKEF
Fontaine Echrob ou Chouf
Mosquée Ben Youssef
RIAD EL AROUS
RUE
BAB DEBBAGH
RUE DE BAB DEBBAGH
Médersa Ben Youssef
Koubba el Baraoudiyn
SOUK
Souk des Forgerons
Souk des Teinturiers
RUE ISSEBTIYNE
SIDI YOUB
BAB AILEN
Zaouïa de Sidi Ben Salah
RUE DE BAB AILEN
RUE SOUK SMARINE
PL. RAHBA KEDIMA
Kissaria
RUE DABACHI
PLACE JEMAA EL FNA
MÉDINA
RUE BAB AHMAD
RUE DOUAR GRAOUA
RUE RIAD ZITOUN EL KEDIM
RUE ZITOUN EL JDID
RUE RIAD
Dar Si Saïd (Musée)
Maison Tiskiwin
AGDAL BA AHMAD
BAB RHEMAT
AVE HOUMMAN EL FETOUAKI
Palais el Bahia
ARSET MAACH
Cimetière de Bab Rhemat
MELLAH
Mosquée d'El Mansour
Palais El Bedi
Tombeaux Saadiens
RUE DE LA KASBAH
Palais Royal
Méchouar
BAB AHMAR
RUE DE BAB AHMAR
BAB KSIBA
RUE DE BAB RHIL
Aguedal
C
D

TOMBEAUX SAADIENS ✪✪

After destroying the neighbouring El-Badi palace, Moulay Ismaïl had the 16th-century tombs of the Saadian rulers sealed off after their ghosts started to appear before him at night. The site, discovered by the French only in 1917, has become a favourite of tour groups, so try and visit late afternoon. The most spectacular of the two mausoleums contains the tomb of Ahmed el-Mansour, the other was built for his mother, father and brother. Scattered around the garden are tombs of many other Saadian royalty.

Once the price is agreed, a calèche is a hassle-free way to discover parts of the medina

- 77C1
- place Yacoub el-Mansour
- 8:30–noon, 2:30–6. Closed Fri AM
- Cheap

A Walk Around Imperial Marrakech

Time
5 hours, avoid lunch time when most sights are closed

Distance
3km

Start point
Bab Aguenaou
77C1

End point
Hotel Mamounia
76B2

Drinks
Cafés on the Jemaa el Fna (£), Hotel Mamounia (£££)

Start at the monumental Bab Aguenaou or the the Gate of the Gnaoua (blacks), from the Almohad reign of Yacoub el-Mansour.

The turquoise minaret and walls of the 12th-century Mosquée d' el-Mansour are straight ahead.

Follow the walls of the mosque to the right for 20m and find to the left the narrow passage leading to the Saadian tombs (► 77). Turn right before Bab Aguenaou gate.

The beautiful Saadien tombs set in a fragrant garden with herbs and blossoms

Walk for 200m, then turn right at the little roundabout towards busy place des Ferblantiers.

At the square, turn right towards Bab Berrima and find through the arch the entrance to El Badi palace (► 74).

Return to the square and on the opposite side in the right corner find the Palais el Bahia (► 75), next to Restaurant de la Bahia.

Back on riad Zitoun el-Jdid, turn right for Maison Tiskiwin (► 75) and the Dar Si Saïd Museum (► 74).

Return to the main street and continue to the end, taking a left at the fork into the rue des Banques and left again to the Jemaa el Fna (► 19).

Walk southwest to place Youssef Ben Tachfine and follow avenue Houmann el-Fetouaki for 300m to reach the Hotel Mamounia (► 105) for a drink on the terrace.

What to See in the High Atlas

Two lavishly decorated rooms remain of the Glaoui palace at Telouet

ASNI (➤ 83)

IMLIL ✪✪

The 17km road and dirt track from Asni to Imlil follows the Oued Reraïa's fertile valley along the river to North Africa's highest mountains, the Jbel Toubkal (➤ 18). The lovely village of Imlil (1740m) is the most popular base for trekking in these mountains. Several offices offer experienced guides, sell maps and hire equipment or mules.

- 72C3
- 17km from Asni
- Nov–May only experienced trekkers above snow line, Feb–Mar danger of flash floods and flooding rivers
- Café Soleil (£)
- Walk, lift or occasional grand taxi

JBEL TOUBKAL (➤ 18, TOP TEN)

OUIRGANE ✪

The landscape is perhaps less dramatic here, but it is still gorgeous and the lovely village makes a perfect base for easier hikes or horse-riding in the region. A 7-hour walk leads through the stunning Nfis gorges to Amizmiz.

- 72C3
- 63km south of Marrakech
- Restaurant (£–££)
- Bus Marrakech–Taroudannt
- Souk Tue

OUKAÏMEDEN ✪✪

At 2,650m, Oukaïmeden ('the meeting place of four winds'), is a popular ski resort. Although most of the resort closes for the summer, it still makes an excellent base for hiking. The approach to Jbel Toubkal is easier than from Imlil. A map available at the Club Alpin chalet shows the whereabouts of fascinating prehistoric rock carvings.

- 72C3
- 72km south of Marrakech
- Resort practically closed in summer
- Auberge Chez Juju (££)
- Grands taxis from Marrakech

TELOUET ✪✪

The crumbling Telouet kasbah (1934) was the headquarter of the notorious el-Glaoui brothers, who ruled south Morocco during the French protectorate. T'Hami el-Glaoui who became the powerful pasha of Marrakech until he was exiled in 1956, befriended the rich and famous, and became renowned for his lavish parties. At his death his Marrakech home, Dar el-Glaoui, was seriously damaged and some of his staff were lynched.

- 72C3
- 21km east off the Tizi-n-Tichka (➤ 82)
- Guardian has the key
- Auberge (£)
- Buses from Marrakech and Ouarzazate stop at the turn-off, 21km from the kasbah

Food – a Cuisine of the Heart

Food in Morocco is a women's affair, an affair of the heart. If Moroccans are seen in expensive Moroccan restaurants, there is usually a social reason for it. Otherwise they'll stay at home, where, everyone is agreed, the best Moroccan food is served. Even the celebrated Mr Boujemaa Mars, head chef at the Mamounia Hotel, Marrakech, admits that however refined he makes his couscous, he much prefers the one his wife prepares at home, because he can never put that much love in his food.

A delicious couscous with seven vegetables is often served to round off a meal

The Food of Love

'If someone created the night for us to dream, then our mothers founded the kitchen to keep our love... Anyone can prepare a dish. But to give love in the use of spices, the flavours and the subtlety, is only within reach of those close to the dreams created by the night.'

From Tahar Ben Jelloun's introduction to *Les saveurs et les gestes* by Fatéma Hal (Paris, 1995)

According to tradition the best cuisine comes from Fès, not surprising since Fès was also home to many wealthy families. In big houses, black *dadas* were – and often still are – the mistresses of the kitchen. These *dadas* belong to a Morocco which tourists rarely see, inhabiting the world behind studded doors and beautiful walls. These master chefs are locally famous and much in demand, while in imperial times, rich Fassis would even take them as their concubine or fourth wife, though their ancestors were probably slaves imported from the Sudan.

A Typical Moroccan Meal

If you don't get a chance to sample home cooking, make a point of visiting one of the better restaurants. Food is often served at low round tables and dishes are usually shared. The meal may start with *harira*, a rich soup of meat and chick peas, often served the Fassi way with dates. A selection of salads, from sweet carrots with rose water to

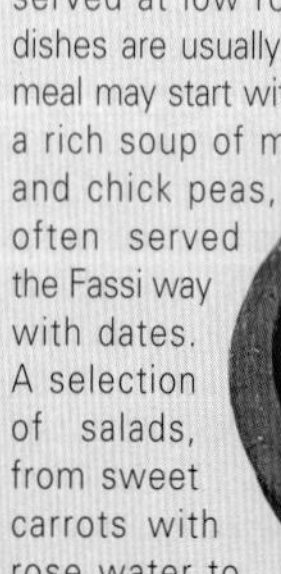

Fish or meat tagines *combined with bitter olives or sweet fruits never fail to surprise the western palate*

One of the best and cheapest souvenirs to take back is a good range of spices

spicy lamb brains will follow, and maybe also a *pastilla* – delicious sweet pastry stuffed with pigeon and almonds. Next comes the *mechoui*, a roasted tender whole lamb or brochettes, followed by the main dish, either a *tagine*, a stew of fish or meat with fruit or olives, or a *couscous*, a delicious mound of semolina cooked with vegetables and mutton. *Khobz* (bread), eaten with the right hand only, is served with everything and in some houses takes the place of cutlery. To end the meal? Some pastries, of which the *Cornes de Gazelles* are the most famous, served with a sweet, digestive *thé à la menthe*.

A Melting Pot of Spices

Spices are the secret, so head for the picturesque spice souk. Prices are cheap so indulging is no sin. 'Ras el-Hanout', literally 'the head of the shop', is a mixture of about 30 spices used in winter dishes to heat the blood. That mixture sums up the different influences on Moroccan cuisine: India (cardamon, cinnamon and long pepper), Guinea (pepper), Africa (Cyparacée), Zanzibar (cloves), Damascus (rose buds), Europe (ash berries) and so on. Other popular spices are cumin, cloves, cinnamon, hot red pepper, sweet red pepper, saffron and aniseed.

Wine and Beer

As Morocco is an Islamic country, the consumption of alcohol is not encouraged. Though some good wines are produced around Meknès, it can be hard to find them outside bars, tourist restaurants and hotels. Alcohol is often prohibited in medinas or close to mosques. Moroccan beers – Stork or the more common Special Flag – are standard pilsners.

Thé à la Menthe
Moroccans seem unable to live without mint tea, a concoction of Chinese green tea, fresh mint and plenty of sugar. More than a mere refreshment, it is a friendly hand shake, brings good luck (green is the colour of Islam) and is a blessing for good health. The tea ceremony is often elaborate with tea poured from great height to ensure it is all well mixed. How can one refuse?

72C2
102km south of Marrakech
Sunrise–sunset, look for the *guardien*. Closed during Fri prayers
Buses from Marrakech to Taroudannt
Cheap. Remember to tip the guardian

Above: *Tin-Mal, one of the only mosques open to non-Muslims*

TIN-MAL

From the road the Great Mosque of Tin-Mal rises high up like a fortress. This is one of the few mosques in Morocco where non-Muslims can enter (find the guardian). Ibn Tumert, founder of the Almohad dynasty, began preaching his puritanical reform movement here in the 12th century and trained Berber tribes to fight anyone who rejected his theories. After his death in 1130, his successor moved to Marrakech and the Almohads became a dynasty. The recently restored mosque is now roofless but the shadow play on its walls only adds to its beauty. In the centre of the village is a ruined kasbah and a small Koranic school.

TIZI-N-TEST (➤ 22–3, TOP TEN)

72C3
204km long
Buses Marrakech–Taroudannt or grands taxis

TIZI-N-TICHKA

The direct route from Marrakech to Ouarzazate is modern, relatively fast and less dramatic than the Tizi-n-Test (➤ 22–3), but the views at 2,260m are still spectacular. The road goes through small villages and Berber settlements and passes the great Glaoui kasbah of Telouet.

72C3
40km south of Marrakech
Auberge Ramuntzo (££) in Arhbalou
Buses from Bab er-Rob in Marrakech

VALLÉE DE L'OURIKA

This delightful mountain valley is a popular excursion from Marrakech. Dar Caid Ourika has a big market on Monday but it can get crowded when the tour buses arrive. The grassland across the river from Setti Fatma is a favourite picnic spot, while a 30-minute walk uphill (behind the first café) leads to the Seven Cascades, a series of waterfalls. The area is notorious for floods, especially in early spring.

A Drive from Marrakech to Tin-Mal

Leaving Marrakech on the road to Asni and Agadir, a sign announces if the Tizi-n-Test (➤ 22–3) is open or closed.

The road to Asni is lined with olive and eucalyptus trees. The snowtopped peaks of Jbel Toubkal (➤ 18) soon appear gloriously ahead. About 30km from Marrakech is the village of Tahanaoute, the first of many villages which appear to have grown organically out of the rock (Tuesday market). Asni, after 50km, has a thriving Saturday souk.

Beyond Grand Hotel du Toubkal (➤ 105) a signpost left points out the road to Imlil (➤ 79), but continue straight through the pine forests towards Ouirgane (➤ 79).

Distance
104km (one way)

Time
3 hours (one way)

Start point
Marrakech
✚ 72C3

End point
Tin-Mal
✚ 72C2

Lunch
Au Sanglier qui Fume (£–££), Ouirgane

The mountains still dominate the region, but the landscape gets gradually wilder and more dramatic.

The Tizi-n-Test road follows the Nfiss river (full of trout in spring) through the steep hills dotted with tiny terraced hamlets and orchards.

Weaving carpets for the ever-increasing number of visitors of Imlil

The hamlet of Ijoujak, after around 90km, is a good base for hiking in the lovely Agoundis Valley.

At the village of Souk al-Arbaa Yaqout, after 100km, take a right at the fork, and the Agadir-n-Gouf (beginning 20th century) on the hilltop is straight ahead to the left of the road.

To the right of the road are the ruins of the impressive Goudafa kasbah of Talaat-n-Yacoub. One kilometre further a small signpost points to Tin-Mal (➤ 82) as its well-restored mosque becomes visible from the road.

A movable feast: the colour of the sand dunes of Erg Chebbi changes with the light

What to See in the South

72C3
30km northwest of Ouarzazate
A guide may be useful to see some of the interiors of the kasbahs
La Kasbah (£) new village, good lunches or Auberge el-Ouidane (£) with excellent views
Grands taxis from Ouarzazate
Free

AÏT-BENHADDOU

The impregnable fortress, with high red *pisé* walls and towers, is deservedly one of the most popular sights in the Atlas. Many Hollywood movies have been filmed here (*Lawrence of Arabia, Jesus of Nazareth* and *The Jewel of the Nile*, to name but a few), as well as countless fashion and advertising shoots. The kasbahs used to command the old road from Marrakech to Ouarzazate, but lost their importance when the French built the new road through the Tizi-n-Tichka. A few families still inhabit the village, living mainly off the tourist trade.

72B1
100km inland from Guelmime
Look for the guardian
Café by the waterfall (£).
No public transport, few trucks on market days

AMTOUDI (ID AÏSSA)

Built on a rock pinnacle, the *agadir* (communal fortified granary) at Amtoudi is one of the oldest and most impressive in the region. The nomadic Iznaguen tribe stored their grain, dates, gunpowder and other valuables here and added a beautiful portal for extra safety. Go for a walk in the palm-lined gorge to find another ruinous *agadir* and, after 3km, a waterfall and café.

73D3
Dadès Valley (➤ 24), 95km east of Ouarzazate
Wed souk (also Wed for Boumalne). Rose festival late May–early June
Restaurant in Hotel des Roses du Dadès (£–££)
Bus to Ouarzazate and Erfoud

EL-KELAA-M'GOUNA

If you are travelling in spring you will find your path lined with pink roses. A rose festival is held here every year to celebrate the harvest, but the shops sell the *eau de rose* and dried roses all year round. A visit to one of the rose-water factories is an interesting and perfumed affair.

El-Kelaa is a good base for exploring the Vallée des Roses to the north or the nearby Boumalne de Dadès and the stark but wildly beautiful volcanic peaks of Jbel Saghro.

73E3
290km east of Ouarzazate

ERFOUD

Built in the 1930s by the French Foreign Legion as the administrative centre of the Tafilalt, Erfoud is a perfect

base for exploring the more remote Berber ksar villages. The Bodj Est, on the town square, commands magnificent views over the palmeries with over 700,000 palm trees. Rissani (22km south), the birthplace of the founder of the Alaouite dynasty, borders the ruins of Sijilmassa. This legendary town, founded in 707, gained importance and prosperity as a post on the major trade route from Niger to Tanger. Further on is a ruined 19th-century Alouite palace, the Ksar Akbar, the shrine of the founder of the reigning Alouite dynasty Moulay Ali Cherif, (closed to non-Muslims) and the Ksar Ouled Abdelhalim, the governor's palace.

- Sun souk
- Best meals in Hotel Salaam on the road to Rissani (££)
- Bus to Er-Rachidia, Rissani
- Oct date festival

ERG CHEBBI ✪✪

A superb ridge of golden sand dunes stretching into the vast Sahara. There is not much else to see but more than enough for a treat. A walk across the dunes at dusk or dawn is a must. Alternatively, try a camel excursion from the Auberge La Grande Dune.

- 73E3
- 61km southeast of Erfoud
- Good bird-watching in spring
- Auberge (££)
- Taxis from Rissani

ER-RACHIDIA ✪

Another town established by the French Foreign Legion, around a 19th-century ksar, there is little of interest here, but this is a good place from which to visit the palm oasis of Figuig on the Algerian border. Figuig has seven *ksour*, the most interesting being Ksar Zenaga, with good views.

- 73E3
- 358km south of Fès
- Sun souk
- Restaurant (££)
- Buses to Figuig, Erfoud, Midelt, Tinerhir, Fès and Meknès
- Flights to Fès
- October date *moussem*

Did you know ?

Ksour are fortified tribal villages. As there is a shortage of building materials, ksour (singular: ksar) are usually built of pisé, *the mud-clay found on riverbanks. They are massive structures with fabulous decorations, often commanding the landscape around but they are vulnerable to rains and need constant upkeep to survive.*

The Todra Gorges are best seen at dawn or dusk, when the soft sunlight produces a palette of pinks, purples and reds

- 73D3
- 70km northeast of Ouarzazate
- La Kasbah (£–££)
- Buses from Tinerhir to Ouarzazate, Boumalne and Er-Rachidia; grands taxis or vans to the gorge
- Tuesday souk

GORGES DU TODRA (OUED TODRA) ✪✪✪

Like the Oued Dadès (➤ 24), the Oued Todra flows out of the High Atlas mountains through a narrow and striking gorge. The Todra gorge is shorter than the Dadès but in some ways is more spectacular. In the deepest, narrowest part of the gorge, past Hotel Mansour, the canyon walls rise a steep 300m above the riverbed, cutting off the sun. The area is perfect for long hikes, but most visitors just come to enjoy the inspiring natural beauty of the gorge, best seen at dawn or dusk, when colours change quickly in a play between sun and shadow, or by the light of a full moon.

The administrative centre is Tinerhir, a pleasant town on a high bank of the Todra, with staggering views over the palmeries. The population is mainly from the Aït Atta tribe, and another ruined Glaoui kasbah towers over the the town. Several well-preserved kasbahs are scattered among these palm groves. Set in the rough hills above the road are a few abandoned *agadirs*. The kasbah of Amitane is one of the most interesting, with Berber brick-and-tile decoration. The source near the Zaouia of Sidi Abdelali is said to cure infertility.

GUELMIME (GOULIMINE) ✪

Because of its camel souk attended by the nomadic 'blue men', Guelmime has become a popular day-trip from Agadir. An important trading post on the Saharan salt-route from the 8th century onwards, tourism is Guelmime's main business today. During the *moussems* (religious festivals) in June and August (moveable dates), the genuine Touaregs come to town.

- 72A1
- 185km south of Agadir
- Camel souk on Sat AM
- Restaurant (£)
- Buses to Agadir, Marrakech; grands taxis to Tan-Tan and Tarfaya

A real blue man eyes up a camel before the next busload of tourists arrives from Agadir

LA'YOUNNE ✪

The Moroccan government has invested heavily in La'younne, capital of the Western Sahara, the former Spanish Sahara, occupied by Morocco in 1975 after the Green March (► 11). The town has an airport, a glittering town centre and an amazing number of offices. The lagoon enclosed by sand dunes is the best sight in town.

- 28B3
- 660km south of Agadir
- Buses to Agadir, Guelmime, Tarfaya, Tan-Tan
- Flights to Agadir, Casablanca, Dakhla

MHAMID ✪

Mhamid is the very extremity of the fertile Dra Valley (► 90). Once an important trading post for the trans-Saharan trade, it declined when the Morocco/Algeria border closed. The new town, built to settle the nomads, has little to offer. Head for the palm groves and picturesque ksour around Mhamid. Jeeps and camels take tourists to the sand dunes of Erg Sedrat or Chegaga.

- 73D2
- 255km south of Zagora
- Hotel Sahara (£)
- Bus from Zagora, or taxi
- Monday souk

OUARZAZATE ✪✪

Ouarzazate is a modern town, administrative capital for the southeast of Morocco and a popular tourist resort. Its dry, hot climate and its well-connected position makes it an ideal base for exploring the south. The only historic building in town is the 19th-century Taourirt Kasbah, a relic of the days when the Glaoui ruled the oases. Inside are craft workshops and two decorated rooms (daily 8–6).

- 73D3
- 204km southeast of Marrakech
- Buses from Marrakech, Tinerhir, Tazanakht, Taliouine, Taroudannt, Agadir, Zagora

- 73E3
- 23km south of Er-Rachidia, 56km north of Erfoud
- Dawn to dusk
- Café (£)
- Buses and grands taxis between Erfoud and Er-Rachidia
- Cheap

SOURCE BLEUE DE MESKI

The Meski River, part of the Ziz Valley system, flows clear and cool out of a cave. One of the French Foreign Legion's happier legacies is a concrete tank, built, so the story goes, to give them bilharzia-free water, where you can swim amongst the carp. A great experience, but one you will probably be sharing – this is one of *the* stopping points in the region for Moroccans and foreigners and tents are sometimes as numerous as palm trees. The ruined Meski ksour can be visited.

- 72B2
- 144km southeast of Agadir
- Restaurants (£–££)
- Daily bus to Agadir and Tiznit

TAFRAOUT

While the Ameln River keeps the valley green, the mountains here are red and purple. Tafraout is the valley's main town, a good base for walking or driving in the region. Its traditional Berber houses are surrounded by palms, olive and almond trees (the February almond blossom festival is the town's biggest attraction).

Several of the weirdly shaped rocks have been given names – Napoleon's Hat and the Carved Gazelle – while 3km away are the blue and red painted rocks of Agard Oudad, the work of Belgian artist Jean Verame.

Right: *the blue contemporary art of Jean Verame doesn't look out of place*

- 72C2
- 200km east of Agadir
- Ask to see the kasbah
- Restaurant (££), auberge (£)
- Buses to Taroudannt and Ouarzazate
- Free, but offer something if shown around kasbah

TALIOUINE

Famed as the source of Morocco's best saffron, Taliouine is often bypassed on the road from Taroudannt to Ouarzazate. The great ruins of the Glaoui kasbah, on the valley floor outside the village, are rarely visited. Families who once served the Glaoui still live in and around the kasbah, as well as in the other villages and kasbahs perched along the sides of the beautiful, almond-lined valley.

Left: *deep-coloured rock formations are a dramatic background to villages in the Ameln Valley*

TAMGROUT ✪✪

Come to fortified Tamgrout, along the Draa valley, to understand something about Moroccan culture: a long way from the glamour of the northern cities, this village was part of the reformist movement which created the 11th-century Almoravid dynasty. The main attraction is its religious complex built around the tomb of the founder of the Naciri brotherhood which includes a medersa and a library of Korans, histories and scientific works, some dating to the 12th century and written on gazelle skins. Happily, for once non-Muslims are allowed in.

- 73D2
- 22km south of Zagora
- Library: 8:30–noon, 3–6. Closed Fri
- Hotel Riad Nacir (£–££)
- Bus to Zagora and Mhamid
- Library: donation welcome

TARHAZOUT (► 54)

TAROUDANNT ✪✪

- 72B2
- 80km east of Agadir
- Hotel Palais Salam 852312
- Souk: best visited in the mornings. Closed Fri
- Cafés (£), restaurants (£–£££)
- Buses to Agadir, Ouarzazate and Marrakech

Behind the golden walls of Taroudannt hides a small town full of charm

While many of Morocco's towns and cities have preserved their walls, Taroudannt is unusual for having kept much of its development within the fortifications: step out of some of the gates and you walk straight into orchards or olive groves, with the snowcapped Atlas Mountains behind. Taroudannt, sitting on one of the main Saharan routes, is the largest market in the Sous Valley and while its souk isn't as exotic as Marrakech or Fès, it is an excellent place to look for Berber jewellery and crafts. The Berber market is off Place Talmoklate.

TIZNIT ✪

Tiznit was created in the 19th century as a new provincial capital. It is a charmingly sleepy place, known for its metalwork (the Jewish jewellers have gone but standards are still high in the jewellers' souk off the Mechouar), blue sultans and a woman called Lalla. Lalla was a reformed prostitute whose death, according to local tradition, was marked by the gushing of a new sweetwater spring.

- 72B2
- 91km south of Agadir
- Cafés and restaurants (£–££)
- Buses up and down the coast
- Tourist information, Sahat el Méchouar (869199)

VALLÉE DU DADÈS (► 24, TOP TEN)

73D2
Restaurants and cafés (£–££)
Buses and grands taxis between Ouarzazate and Mhamid
Tourist information, Sahat el Méchouar (869199); Avenue Mohammed V, Ouarzazate (88248)

Trésor du désert: *treasures of the desert, or a carpet shop too many?*

VALLÉE DU DRA

One of the great natural spectacles of Morocco, the Oued Dra flows out of the Anti-Atlas and south into the desert. In years of heavy rainfall it used to run all the way to the Atlantic, but its flow is now controlled by the Barrage el-Mansour Eddahabi and it only just makes it to Mhamid.

Beyond Agdz, 68km south of Ouarzazate, (famous for brightly coloured Berber carpets), the valley today is lined with kasbahs and ksour, as it was in the time of the Saadian sultans. The ksar of Tamnougalt and kasbah of Timiderte, are among the most impressive. Zagora (below) is usually as far as most people travel, though the road continues through Tamgrout (► 89) and the sand dunes of Tinfou, to Mhamid (► 87).

73D2
168km southeast of Ouarzazate
Restaurant (££)
Buses to Ouarzazate and Mhamid; camel excursions from La Fibule du Draa, in Amazrou
Important *moussem* of Moulay Abdelkader Jilala. Souk held Wed and Sun

ZAGORA

Zagora reflects none of the beauty of the land around it, although the oasis has been inhabited for centuries and it was from here that the Saadians began their conquest of Morocco. The French made Zagora an administrative town and it is now a useful base, with a range of hotels and restaurants. Good walks to an Almoravid fortress and to the 'Jewish kasbah' at Amazraou (the Jews have gone), but Zagora's most famous sight is the signpost 'Tombouctou 52 jours', marking a start point of the old Saharan camel caravans.

Where To...

The North

Prices
Prices are for a three-course meal for two without drinks.
£ = less than 250 dirham
££ = 250–450 dirham
£££ = more than 450 dirham

Asilah

Casa Garcia (££)
Fish specialities served on a seafront terrace overlooking the new harbour.
✉ 51 rue Moulay Hassan-Ben-el-Mehdi ☎ 917465 ⌚ Lunch, dinner

Chez Pepe (Oceano) (££)
People come specially from Tanger for the fresh fish and relaxed service. Swordfish is a speciality and the house wine is good.
✉ place Zellaka ☎ 917395 ⌚ Lunch, dinner

Cap Spartel

Le Mirage (££)
Stunning views over the sea and good choice of fish and seafood from a simple red mullet to shark and lobster. A cosy room inside with fireplace for the winter evenings. Recommended.
✉ Above the grottoes in Cap Spartel ☎ 333332 ⌚ Lunch, dinner 🚖 Grand taxi from the place du 9-Avril-1947 in Tanger

Chechaouen

Casa Hassan/Tissemlal (£)
The best Moroccan food in town with little *amuse-gueules* to start. Hassan loves food and has an eye for interior design as well.
✉ Pension Chez Hassan, 22 rue Targhi ☎ 986153 ⌚ Lunch, dinner

Granada (£)
Equally good food but only two choices: couscous or *tagine*. Very relaxed, family atmosphere.
✉ rue Targhi, further up the street ⌚ Lunch, dinner

Zouar (£)
Small but good Spanish restaurant specialising in fish and seafood. No alcohol.
✉ 30m from the post office going up towards rue Moulay-Ali-Ben-Rachid ⌚ Lunch, dinner (paella must be ordered a few hours in advance)

Larache

Al-Khozama (££)
Excellent cuisine prepared by a prize-winning chef.
✉ 114 avenue Mohammed V ☎ 914454 ⌚ Lunch, dinner

Restaurant (without a name) (£)
Grilled meat or liver served with chakchouka, a North African ratatouille with eggs and olives, and bread for near to nothing.
✉ rue Ibn Batouta ⌚ All day

Martil

La Playa (££)
Good fish, especially grilled swordfish. Great view.
✉ At the beach ⌚ Lunch and dinner

Melilla

Bar El Rincón (£)
Good brochettes and wine.
✉ rue Lopez-Moreno ⌚ All day

Heladería Alaska
Best ice-cream on the northern coast. Worth a detour.
✉ 1st street right walking up avenue du Generalísimo ⌚ All day

Tanger

Café de Paris (£)
Great terrace from which to watch all of Tanger (if not all the world) pass by. People move between this café and the Café de France across the square according to the position of the sun.

place de France **Morning until late evening**

Café Hafa (£)
Popular café, tricky to find, with startling views over Tanger and the sea. A favourite with many Tanger residents including the writer Paul Bowles, this is a perfect place to while away the afternoon over a mint tea or two. Worth the search!
quartier Marshan, in an alley at the back of the stadium, ask for directions everyone knows it **Morning until late evening**

Caïds Bar (££)
Long-established bar with a dedicated following of resident ex-pats and eccentrics. Good cocktail and champagne list. In summer, sit in the beautiful garden.
El-Minzah Hotel, 85 rue de la Liberté **938787** **Daily noon–evenings**

El-Korsan (££–£££)
The best Moroccan restaurant in town, with elegant food in Fès style. Excellent pastilla and couscous Fassi, served in luxurious surroundings.
El-Minzah Hotel, 85 rue de la Liberté **935885** **Daily lunch, dinner**

Garden Restaurant Guitta's
Formerly one of Tanger's most select and secretive restaurants, but no more. After thirty years this place is only recommended for nostalgics who want to savour the last smelly breath of a Tanger that has otherwise disappeared.
110 Sidi Bouabid **937333** **Daily lunch and dinner**

Marhaba (££)
Delicious Moroccan dishes served in a baroque room full of colours, with live music to stir the appetites.
67 rue de la Kasbah, opposite the entrance to the Kasbah, Medina **937643** **Daily lunch, dinner**

Raihari (£–££)
Traditional Moroccan cuisine served by friendly waiters. The *couscous au poulet* is great.
10 rue Ahmed Chaouki **934866** **Daily lunch, dinner**

Romero (££)
Choice paella and wonderful fish specialities served in an unremarkable Andalucian décor.
12 avenue Prince Moulay Abdallah **932277** **Daily lunch, dinner**

San Remo (Chez Toni) (££)
In a bright, simply-decorated room, choose from a wide variety of international dishes. Don't miss the tartes at the end.
15 rue Ahmed-Chaouki **938451** **Tue–Sun lunch and dinner. Closed Mon**

Tetouan

Le Restinga (£)
Good value, tasty Moroccan meals and efficient service.
21 rue Mohammed V **Daily lunch, dinner**

Zarhoun (££)
Richly decorated room, Moroccan music and a small but well-prepared menu make this the best restaurant in town.
boulevard Mohammed-Ben-Larbi-Torrès **Daily lunch, dinner**

Tanger, a City of Bars
'Dean's Bar stood, as it were, midway from the Mountain with its cliques and genteel tribalism, to the Bar la Mar Chica with its dockside slumming and picturesque 'low life'. Between them came the more bourgeois resorts, the Parade Bar, Madame Porte's café, and the various little upstart bars which Englishmen, chiefly in pairs, opened up to earn a living by bringing together their fellow countrymen and the young Moors ...'
Rupert Croft-Cooke, quoted in Iain Finlayson's excellent *Tangier, City of the Dream* (London, 1992)

The Atlantic Coast

Order in Advance

Moroccan cuisine takes ages to prepare and a lifetime to get it absolutely right. Most restaurants offer the standards – harira, tagines with chicken and olives and couscous – but specialities like *mechoui* or roast lamb or a whole grilled fish or fish tagine need to be ordered in advance, and usually for at least 2 people. If planning on a splurge for dinner, call or visit the restaurant beforehand and your wish will be their command.

Agadir

Azzahra (£)

This restaurant specialises in couscous with cinnamon as well as fried calamari and other delicious Moroccan dishes, served on a pleasant terrace.

✉ 60 avenue du Prince Moulay-Abdallah, behind cinema Rialto 🕐 Lunch, dinner

La Caverne (£)

Cheaper than most but good quality food served in a European décor. Very popular with Gadiris.

✉ Résidence Mer et Soleil, boulevard Hassan II 🕐 Lunch, dinner

Le Jardin d'Eau (££)

Delicious French food and Moroccan dishes. The speciality is *mechoui*.

✉ boulevard du 20 Août ☎ 840195 🕐 Lunch, dinner

La Maison du Pain (£)

Large choice of delicious pastries and freshly squeezed fruit juices served here, as well as good ice-creams.

✉ 19 avenue Hassan II, Assima building near the Hotel Petite Suède ☎ 840739 🕐 All day

Le Miramar (£££)

This Italian restaurant specialises in fish, seafood and pasta dishes. The food is excellent and the Italian patron is never short of a story.

✉ boulevard Mohammed V ☎ 840770 🕐 Lunch, dinner

Palm Beach, Chez Roger (££)

Healthy cooking with an attractive selection of salads, as well as grilled fish and meat. View of the sea and beach.

✉ On the beach near Club Med 🕐 Lunch, dinner

La Pergola (££)

Madame Mirabel runs this French restaurant. Very seventies, with Provençal décor and huge flower bouquets, it feels a long way from Morocco. Huge menu with all the classics and very attentive service.

✉ Km.8, Route Agadir-Inezgane (8km from Agadir centre) ☎ 830841 🕐 Lunch, dinner

La Tour de Paris (£££)

Elegant restaurant with good French cuisine, both traditional and *nouvelle cuisine*. Reservation is advisable.

✉ avenue Hassan II ☎ 840906 🕐 Lunch, dinner. Closed Sat

Casablanca

Al-Mounia (££–£££)

One of Casa's most pleasant restaurants set in a Moroccan pavillion with garden serving superb dishes. The pastilla is close to divine.

✉ 95 rue du Prince-Moulay-Abdallah ☎ 222669 🕐 Daily lunch, dinner

A Ma Bretagne (£££)

Classic French cuisine prepared by *maître cuisinier* André Halbert, this is Casablanca's best and most expensive. Elegant interior and great views of the beach and sea. Worth every dirham!

✉ boulevard Sidi-Abderrahmane, 8km out of town ☎ 362112 🕐 Mon–Sat lunch, dinner. Closed Sun

L'Auberge Bavaroise (£–££)
Large choice of good French dishes prepared by a chef from Marseilles. Friendly service, cosy decor.
129 rue Allal-Ben-Abdallah 311760 Daily lunch, dinner

Bar Casablanca (£££)
Trying hard to re-create the atmosphere of 'Rick's Bar' in the movie 'In Bar Casablanca' the waiters dress in Bogart-style trenchcoats and fedoras, the walls are covered with posters and pictures from the film.
Hyatt Regency, place Mohammed V 261234 Morning till evening

Le Cabestan (£££)
One of the city's best fish restaurants in a villa overlooking the sea. If this one is full try the equally good La Mer next door (363315).
boulevard de la Corniche, near the el-Hank lighthouse 391190 Lunch, dinner. Closed Sun

L'Etoile Marocaine (£)
Almost next door to the Bavaroise, good Moroccan food served in salons with low tables. No alcohol served here.
107 rue Allal-Ben-Abdallah 314100 Daily lunch, dinner

Le Petit Poucet (£)
Now a rather cheap and friendly restaurant, this used to be one of the best places to eat in Casablanca when French pilot-writer Antoine de Saint-Exupéry was passing through town. His letters decorate the walls and still draw his fans. Food for nostalgics.
86 boulevard Mohammed V 275420 Lunch, dinner

Le Port de Pêche (££–£££)
Excellent address for fresh fish dishes prepared to your choice. The décor is simple and the fish is brought to the table before being cooked. The fish soup is memorable.
In the Port de Pêche (fishing harbour), go towards the customs and turn left before the gate, then go straight until the police station 318561 Daily lunch, dinner, book in advance

Villa Fandango (££)
Meeting place for Casablanca's well-heeled youth, therefore always crowded, and with an extraordinary atmosphere. There is salsa, flamenco, tapas and Mexican Sol beer, and a doorman who won't let you in unless you're well-dressed.
rue Hubert Giron, from the Corniche turn left before Croc Magnon restaurant 398508 Evenings

El-Jadida

Restaurant of the Hotel de Provence (££)
French-Moroccan cuisine served in a pleasant atmosphere. Garden terrace.
42 avenue Fquih Mohammed er-Rafi 342347 Lunch, dinner

Safari Pub (£)
Appetising *menu du jour* and standards like fresh grilled sardines or octopus salad with a glass of beer or wine.
6–8 avenue Fquih Mohammed er-Rafi Lunch, dinner

Recommended Cookery Books
Fez, Traditional Moroccan Cooking, Z Guinaudeau, translated by J E Harris (J E Laurent, Rabat)
Les Saveurs et les Gestes, Cuisines et Traditions du Maroc, Fatéma Hal (Stock, Paris)
Secrets of Moroccan Cooking and Moroccan Cooking – the Best Recipes, Fetouma Benkirane, translated by Shirley Kay (Sochepress)

Eat Like a Berber
If you get fed up with the usual restaurant fare, try Essaouira's so-called *café-berbères*. In the small square at the end of the jewellery souk there are several cafés, the cleanest and best being Mamma Fatima's (the sign on the door reads 'Chez la mamma'). Choose what you like in the market and tell her how to cook it, or order in advance and let her do the shopping. Apparently mamma Fatima used to work in a big restaurant in town.

Essaouira

Chalet de la Plage (££)

This fish restaurant, run by the same family for over 25 years and with a terrace overlooking the sea, is an Essaouira institution. The décor is that of a classic 1960s fish restaurant with nets, boats and wood-panelled walls. The food – fish and seafood, of course – is very well prepared. The more expensive menu with lobster and oysters is extremely good value.

✉ boulevard Mohammed V, on the beach ☎ 473419 🕐 Lunch, dinner

Chez Driss (£)

Old-fashioned pâtisserie kept by the same family since 1925. Good fruit juices and cakes served in a tiny blue-tiled patio. Pastilla or pizza can be ordered in advance.

✉ 10 rue Hajjali, off the place Moulay el-Hassan 🕐 All day

Chez Sam/Restaurant du Port (££)

Overlooking the busy fishing harbour, the fish and seafood don't have far to travel to arrive fresh on your table. Great fish, good views from the cosy restaurant or the cool terrace upstairs, friendly and sometimes slow service and good-value set menus with lobster. What more could you want?

✉ At the end of the fishing harbour ☎ 473513 🕐 Lunch, dinner

Dar Baba (££)

Impeccable Italian restaurant in an old Souiri house, with simple pasta dishes prepared by an Italian couple.

✉ 2 rue Marrakech 🕐 Lunch, dinner

Dar Loubane (£££)

Most recent arrival in town, a restaurant under French management, on three floors around the patio of an 18th-century riad, serving excellent French and Moroccan food. Very good home-made patisserie.

✉ 24 rue du Rif, near the clock 🕐 Lunch, dinner

Es-Salaam (£–££)

Cosy restaurant with good Moroccan food and specialities of fish *tagines*. The boss is not only a good cook, he adores telling customers about the beauty of Essaouira. Order fish grills or *tagines* well in advance.

✉ place Moulay el-Hassan 🕐 Breakfast, lunch, dinner. Closed during Ramadan

Naturesa (£)

Run by two young Sicilians, who produce their own Italian ice-cream in season, as well as good pizzas or just an espresso to kick off the day.

✉ 1 rue Sidi-Med-Ben-Abdallah 🕐 All day

Imouzzer-Ida-Outanan

Terrace of the Hotel des Cascades (££)

Excellent address to recover from the long but beautiful road from the coast, with a lunch of fresh salads and grilled meat, a cool bottle of wine, and a panoramic view. Highly recommended!

✉ ► 103

Oualidia

A l'Araignée Gourmande (££)

Fish, fish and more fish, not to mention excellent Oualidia

oysters. On weekends book in advance or come early as it gets pretty crowded.
✉ plage du Maroc ⌚ Lunch, dinner

l'Hippocambe (££–£££)
Wonderful restaurant with a quiet terrace under a big tree, overlooking the beach. Specialities of fresh fish brochettes, oysters and lobster. Ideal for a long lunch (kids can play within sight on the beach). Recommended.
✉ On the beach in Oualidia (signposted) ⌚ Lunch, dinner

Rabat

La Caravelle (£–££)
Simple food like brochettes and fried fish are served in this extraordinary location, in the walls of the kasbah, with a magnificent view over the sea, the river and Salé.
✉ Borj de la Kasbah des Oudaïas, just under the panoramic viewpoint ☎ 738844 ⌚ Mid-Jun–late summer, dinner

La Clef (£)
Good value restaurant with Moroccan and French specialities, very good pastillas with almonds or chicken. The décor is homey Moroccan, with banquettes and low tables.
✉ Corner of rue Hatim and avenue Moulay Youssef ☎ 701972 ⌚ Daily lunch, dinner

Dinarjat (£££)
At the beginning of the avenue Laalou, opposite the Kasbah des Oudaïas, a sign indicates the restaurant. From there a porter with a lantern will lead through the curvy alleys of the medina. The traditional Moroccan food is worth the adventure.
✉ 6 rue Belgnaoui, Medina (avenue Laalou) ☎ 704239 ⌚ Daily evenings

Kangourou Grill (££)
Renowned for some of the best grills in Morocco (and excellent carrot cake), served in a décor inspired by Australian Bushmen. Sounds tacky, but the food and the atmosphere are good.
✉ Hotel Shérérazade, 21 rue de Tunis ☎ 722226 ⌚ Daily evenings. Live music on Fri and Sat nights

Lina (£)
Excellent French pastries and pâtisserie served in a Moroccan rarity: a non-smoking café. Recommended for breakfast or afternoon tea.
✉ 45 avenue Allal-Ben-Abdellah ☎ 707291 ⌚ Daily 7AM–9PM

Restaurant de la Plage (££)
Big terrace with view on the sea. Excellent for a peaceful beer and fish specialities.
✉ plage (beach) de Rabat, to the left of the Kasbah des Oudaïas ☎ 723148 ⌚ Daily lunch, dinner

Zerda (also known as Chez Michel) (£)
A great atmosphere and Moroccan Jewish dishes make it worth braving this smoky, crowded place.
✉ 7 rue Patrice Lumumba ☎ 730912 ⌚ Daily lunch, dinner

Safi

Refuge Sidi Bouzid (££)
Delicious fish and seafood overlooking the sea. Very pleasant.
✉ On the road to el-Jadida (3km) ⌚ Lunch, dinner

The Wines of Morocco
Wine is made in three regions: Berkane, Meknès and Boulâouane. Meknès wines are considered the best. Restaurant wine lists are usually quite limited but if you have the choice look out for Gris de Boulâouane, Oustalet rosé, the Special Coquillages and Valpierre Blanc de Blanc white wines and for Cabernet Président red. The best red wine on the market is Beauvallon, but you rarely see it in restaurants. Only a few shops sell alcohol, usually in the more upmarket groceries of the *ville nouvelle* in bigger towns.

Fès Palaces
Several restaurants in old houses or palaces offer expensive meals, often with traditional live music and a belly dancer. It is an impressive experience, but it can be quite artificial. If the place is animated it can be fun, but if it is just the two of you it can be a depressing experience. Call in advance.

Moyen Atlas and Imperial Cities

Azrou

Restaurant of the Hotel des Cèdres
In season, well-prepared European and Moroccan dishes, with cheap and good fish grills.
Main square 562326
Lunch, dinner

Fès

Al-Fassia (£££)
Some of Morocco's best food is served in the splendour of a beautiful hall in the hotel's old palace. Remember that specialities like *mechoui* must be ordered in advance. Excellent Moroccan sweets, especially *cornes de gazelles*.
Palais Jamai hotel
634331/635090 Dinner only with belly dance and music

Al-Jenina (£££)
The French restaurant of the Palais Jamai may have a less atmospheric décor, but the food is excellent and the tables outside in the garden are perfect for a quiet lunch or a romantic dinner.
Palais Jamai
634331/635090 All day

Chez Vittorio (££)
Noisy Italian restaurant with pasta and good meat dishes. Recommended for when you can't face *tagine*.
21 rue Brahim-Redani, opposite the Hotel Central
624730 Lunch, dinner

Dar Saada (££)
One of Fès's better restaurants, in a beautiful converted palace. The location is great for touring the medina, although the number of tour groups seriously disturbs the tranquility. Set menus are good value but the drinks are quite expensive.
21 souk Attarine, Medina
633343 Lunch

Dar Tajine (££–£££)
Another splendid converted palace with Fassi specialities to be ordered in advance. Good food and sharp service. Call beforehand to see if the restaurant is open.
Palais Hadj Omar Lebbar, 15 Ross Rhi, Medina 634161
Daily lunch, dinner

Le Mounia (££)
Good selection of Moroccan and French dishes served in an enjoyable decor. Prices are reasonable and there is air-conditioning in summer.
11 boulevard Mohammed Zerktouni 624838
Lunch, dinner

La Noria (£)
A popular café with young Moroccans, overlooking the gardens, crenallated walls and a broken waterwheel, this is an excellent place to stop before or after Fès el-Bali. A couscous lunch can be eaten if ordered in advance.
I the Bou Jeloud Gardens
625422 All day (evenings also in summer)

Palais de Fès (££–£££)
An elegant 14th-century mansion with a restaurant and a roof terrace overlooking the medina where you can just sip a mint tea or coffee. The Moroccan or French food is usually excellent.
16 Boutouil-Qaraouiyyin, Fès el Bali 634707
Lunch only

Palais M'Nebhi (£££)
In a palace once occupied by the French General Lyautey, Haj Sentissi serves some of the most delicate food in Fès. If you only have one couscous maybe it should be here as it is simply delicious.
450m east of the Boujeloud Gate · Telephone for opening hours

Salon de thé-pâtisserie l'Epi d'Or (£)
Excellent croissants and pâtisseries for breakfast or afternoon coffee, and delicious juices and almond milk.
85 boulevard Mohammed V, Ville Nouvelle · All day

Meknès

Ãnnexe du Métropole 1 (£–££)
Authentic Moroccan food served on low tables surrounded by tiles and stucco work. Not to be confused with the nearby Metropole. Annexe II is near Hotel Transatlantique.
11 rue Charif-Idrissi, next door to the central market · 525668 · Daily lunch, dinner

Le Collier de la Colombe (££)
Modern restaurant with a French/ Moroccan menu with panoramic views over the Jardin Haboul and part of Meknès. Popular with tour groups for lunch.
67 rue Driba · 555041 · Daily lunch, dinner

La Coupole (££)
Well prepared dishes from a mixed French-Moroccan menu served in a wonderfully retro décor. The attached bar is popular.
Corner of avenue HassanII and Zankat Ghana, Ville Nouvelle · 522483 · Daily lunch, dinner

Pizzeria Le Four (££)
Popular with wealthier Meknassis who come to enjoy a really good rectangular pizza with a glass of wine or beer. Also pasta and meat dishes.
1 rue Atlas · 520857 · Lunch, dinner

Zitouna (££)
Great Moroccan restaurant in an old house in the medina with fountains and a beautiful interior. Best in the evening as the atmosphere can be spoilt at lunch time with noisy tour groups.
44 Jamaa Zitouna · 530281 · Daily lunch, dinner

Moulay Idriss

Baraka de Zerhoun (£–££)
A restaurant run by two women who serve simple but tasty *tagines*, Zerhoun olives, fresh butter and good salads. Recommended.(no alcohol)
22 Aïn Smen Khiber, at the top of the village · 544184 · Lunch. Telephone for dinner bookings.

Volubilis

Juba (££)
Excellent Moroccan restaurant with panoramic views of the Roman ruins of Volubilis and the well-maintained garden. The hotel also runs a good international restaurant and a snack bar with terrace.
Hotel Volubilis, Route P28, Zerhoun (near the site of Volubilis) · Daily lunch, dinner

Mineral Water from the Spring

The Moyen Atlas is home to Morocco's best known springs. In Oulmès-les-Thermes both the Oulmès and Sidi Ali sparkling water is bottled. Mineral water emerges here at 43°C and is good for hepatitis, arthritis and anaemia sufferers. Nearer to Fès is Sidi-Harazem where the still water is bottled which is available all over Morocco. Both places have a health hotel.

The High Atlas & The South

A Moroccan Breakfast
Some hotel breakfast buffets include a few Moroccan dishes worth trying out, but beware: they are filling! *Harira*, a rich soup, is often served in winter. *Rghaif* is a kind of bread, shining with grease and coloured with red pepper. Little pancakes are served with butter and local honey. Baguette comes with a date paste or sweet tomato jam.

Er-Rachidia

Imilchil (£)
Traditional cuisine, friendly service and a beautiful garden terrace.
avenue Moulay-Ali-Cherif 572123 Breakfast, lunch, dinner

Erfoud

Les Dunes (£)
Good address for simple but excellent food. The welcoming patron will also organize excursions into the desert with a dinner under the stars and a real *mechoui*.
avenue Moulay Ismaïl 576793 Lunch, dinner

Auberge-kasbah Derkaoua 'Oasis' (£££)
Stunning surroundings and wonderful food, particulary couscous and *tagine* to order. Also home-made ice-creams, gazpacho and more cooling dishes, welcome in the desert heat.
At km 23, on the road to Merzouga, at the end of the tarmac follow the track to the left to the kasbah and fax 577140 Lunch, dinner

Gorges du Todra

Restaurant of the Hotel Les Roches (£–££)
Well-prepared Moroccan food served under beautiful tents and accompanied by melancholic Berber music. Can get crowded at lunch, but the evenings are usually quiet.
In the gorge Lunch, dinner

Marrakech

Bagatelle (££)
Run by a French couple who serve good French country food. In summer, meals are served under the vines in a cool garden.
101 rue de Yougoslavie 430274 Lunch, dinner. Closed Wed and in Sep

Café le Jet d'Eau (£)
Popular and pleasant terrace for a drink or a snack, in a lovely art déco building.
Crossroads of boulevards Mohammed V and Zerktouni All day until late at night

Catanzaro (££)
Another French-run restaurant, specialising in charcoal grills and pizzas, as well as excellent fresh pastas and lasagnes. Worth booking, as it does get full.
rue Tarik-ibn-Ziyad, behind the central market 433731 Lunch, dinner. Closed Sun and in Aug

Chez Jack'Line (££)
Usual French-Moroccan cuisine with some good-value set menus, in an unusual environment, ruled over by a parrot and the transvestite *patronne* Jack'Line.
63 avenue Mohammed V Lunch, dinner

Dar Marjana (£££)
At Dar Majana (the Coral House) you are received with a drink in the courtyard as if this sumptious medina-palace was your own. After that, at one of six tables, an enormous and memorable dinner is served, a succession of dishes, the next even better than the last ... If you only have one 'palace experience' in Morocco, this is the place to come. The fixed price includes unlimited food and drink. Advance booking essential.
Bab Doukala. Someone from the restaurant will lead you 441110/445773

Dinner, dress for the occasion

Dar Yacout (£££)
Same style as the Dar Marjana around an Andalucian pool. Terrace with views of the medina. Fixed price for the evening.
79 Sidi Ahmed Soussi in the medina **Dinner only**

Le Marocain (£££)
The best of Moroccan food in a traditional Moorish setting, with Andalucian band and belly dancers. Charming maître d, world class chef and excellent food: try buffet lunch by the pool or the Italian restaurant with Venetian specialities for dinner.
Hotel La Mamounia, avenue Bab el Jedid **448981**
Dinner 8-midnight, dresscode very formal. Book in advance

Le Pavillion (£££)
A great French restaurant run by a French decorator in this exceptional riad in the medina. The experience is a feast for the tastebuds and the eyes.
47, Derb Zaouïa, near Bab Doukkala **391240**
Dinner. Closed Wed

La Trattoria (£££)
Elegant Italian restaurant where the *beau monde* of Marrakech comes to dine. Décor by Bill Willis who decorated the Tichka hotel.
179 rue Mohammed el-Beqal, Guéliz **432641**
Dinner. Closed Mon

Ouarzazate

Chez Dimitri (£–££)
A former post office, ballroom and petrol station, this is now one of Ouarzazate's best places to eat and drink. Well stocked bar. The restaurant tends to be overwhelmed by tour groups.
avenue Mohammed V
Closed Fri

Essalam (£)
Lively restaurant with sunny terrace offering several set menus. Good place for breakfast too.
avenue du Prince-Héritier Sidi Mohammed **All day**

Taroudannt

Restaurant at Hotel Roudani (£)
Good servings of freshly grilled brochettes, chips and salad at keen prices.
place el-Alaaouyine
Lunch, dinner

Restaurant and bar of the Hotel Taroudannt (£–££)
Good French cuisine, a *pastis* to start the meal and cheese and salads at the end. Shame about the TV.
place Assarag **852416**
Lunch, dinner

Tinerhir

Hotel-Restaurant Le Tombouctou (£)
Delicious Moroccan and French food served under the qaid's tent. The owner, author of a Spanish hiking guide, knows the area well.
avenue Bir-Anzarane
834604 **Lunch, dinner**

Vallée du Dra

Restaurant of Hotel Kissane (££)
Excellent real Moroccan cuisine. No alcohol.
Just before Agdz on the right **843044** **Lunch, dinner**

Zagora

Hotel-Restaurant Kasbah Asma (££)
Two good menus served in the salons under a tent near an enchanting patio with a fountain. Candle-lit dinner is served in the wonderful rose garden. Specialities can be ordered in advance.
2km from the centre, after the bridge over Oued Dra
847241 **Lunch, dinner by candle-light**

The Street Kitchen
At night, the Jemaa el Fna in Marrakech and squares in other Moroccan towns and cities are filled with food stalls. The food is fresh and can be wonderful. There are usually a few people making *merguez* (spicy sausage) sandwiches, *harira* (a hearty soup with meat and vegetables), the eternal brochettes, the popular wild snail soup (boubbouches) or, for the more adventurous, an aphrodisiac cow's foot or a juicy sheep's head.

The North

Prices
Prices are for a standard double room with bathroom and breakfast, taxes included.

£ = **under 450 dirham**
££ = **459–900 dirham**
£££ = **more than 900 dirham**

Agadir

Anezi (£££)
Well-run but huge holiday complex with luxurious rooms overlooking the ocean. Three swimming pools, saunas, tennis courts and all mod-cons as expected.
✉ **boulevard Mohammed V**
☎ **840714, fax 840713**

La Petite Suède (£)
Small hotel with a personal touch, 200m from the beach, with well-kept rooms and a beautiful patio. Rooms on the street side are rather noisy.
✉ **avenue HassanII**
☎ **840779, fax 840057**

Chechaouen

Parador (£££)
Well-situated hotel, a few steps from the Uta el Hammam and souks, tastefully renovated in the eighties. Comfortable rooms with beautiful bathrooms and a terrace recommended for its great views of the mountain.
✉ **rue Tarik-ibn-Ziad**
☎ **986324, fax 987033**

Pension Casa Hassan (£)
Very clean pension and restaurant with a Moroccan interior and a fountain in the courtyard.
✉ **22 rue Targhi** ☎ **986153, fax 988196**

Larache

Grand Hôtel d'Espagne (££)
Wonderful rooms in this Spanish-style building. Rooms overlooking the square are noisier but have good balconies, great for crowd-watching.
✉ **2 avenue HassanII**
☎ **913195**

Tanger

Continental (££)
Delightful old colonial hotel at the edge of the medina, with good views on the sea and the port. Rooms are quite run-down, but the atmosphere and friendly service makes up for it. The terrace is wonderful for a drink late afternoon after visiting the kasbah or the medina.
✉ **36 Dar Baroud, Medina**
☎ **931024, fax 931143**

El-Minzah (£££)
Built in 1930 by the English Lord Bute and decorated in Moorish style, the recently enlarged Minzah is the perfect place to stay in the heart of Tanger. Within near walking distance of the beach, the Kasbah, the medina, the Minzah also has beautiful gardens with views over the town and harbour for those who prefer a more distant image. Good restaurant and bar.
✉ **85 rue de la Liberté/Zankat el-Houriya** ☎ **938787, fax 934546**

Tetouan

Principe (£)
Clean, popular hotel in the centre of town with recently renovated bathrooms. Come early, as it is often booked. Rooms on the top floor don't get hot water.
✉ **20 avenue de la Résistance**
☎ **962795**

Le Safir (£££)
Peaceful hotel with spacious rooms tastefully decorated with Moroccan fabrics and with good balconies.
✉ **avenue Der Far, M'Diq, 3km from the centre** ☎ **970144, fax 970692**

The Atlantic Coast

Casablanca

Guynemer (£)

Friendly, clean hotel in a quiet but central location.
✉ 2 rue Mohammed Balloil ☎ 275764, fax 473999

Royal Mansour (£££)

The most Moroccan in atmosphere of all Casa's five-star hotels, though not without its critics. The winter garden is recommended for a relaxing afternoon drink.
✉ 27, avenue des Forces Armées Royales ☎ 313011, fax: 312583

Touring (£)

Very central hotel with good large rooms with balconies. Book in advance.
✉ 87 rue Allal-Ben-Abdallah ☎ 310216

El-Jadida

Hôtel de Provence (£–££)

By far the most pleasant place to stay, with clean, spacious rooms, good breakfast and an excellent restaurant.
✉ 42 avenue Fquih Mohammed er-Rafi ☎ 342347, fax 352115

Le Palais Andalous (££)

Slightly out of the centre, this converted medersa has retained a lot of character. Beautiful stucco work, *zellig* tiles, marble floors and luxurious rooms in the former cells of the students. Lovely Moorish salons with comfortable sofas. Recommended.
✉ boulevard Docteur de Lannoë ☎ 343735/343906

Essaouira

Auberge Tangaroo (££)

A quiet hotel with simple but beautiful rooms tastefully decorated in Moroccan style. Magnificent surroundings. Popular with windsurfers! Half board compulsory.
✉ 5km out on the road to Agadir

Sidi Kaouiki (££)

Another perfect place for windsurfers or for those looking for a rest. A new hotel with just a few rooms on a spit of sand – beautiful! Half board compulsory.
✉ 20km out on the road to Agadir ☎ fax see Villa Maroc

Villa Maroc (££)

The best place to stay in town, these two riads have been knocked through to offer a wide variety of rooms, tastefully decorated with local crafts and paintings by local painters. Many little corners and salons to relax and read. Excellent breakfast served outside your room or on the panoramic roof terrace.
✉ 10 rue Abdellah-Ben-Yassin ☎ 473147, fax 472806

Imouzzer-Ida-Outanan

Hotel des Cascades (££)

Delightful and friendly hotel with clean, simple rooms (central heating and air-conditioning), a balcony with a view over the valley and a good restaurant (► 96)
✉ Imouzzer-Ida-Outanan ☎ 08-826016 or office in Agadir ☎ 842671, fax 821671

Oualidia

l'Hippocambe (££–£££)

Another of the hidden delights of Morocco's Atlantic coast, this quiet hotel has clean, comfortable rooms in a lovely garden, some with view on the beach and lagoon. Swimming pool. Recommended.
(► 97)

Railway Hotels

The chain of Moussafir hotels (££) offer excellent value (half board included) and are very well kept. Usually built in a modern interpretation of traditional Moroccan architecture, they are usually a notch above other hotels in their category. Conveniently located opposite or near the train stations, they are recommended if you are travelling by train, though the down side is that the rooms can be quite noisy.

Palace Hotels
Morocco has a few grand hotels, often old palaces in an excellent central location. The most remarkable view from a balcony window is undoubtedly in the Palais Jamai, with all of Fès el Bali at your feet, seen through the palm trees of the hotel's Andalucian garden. The Mamounia, Africa's most luxurious hotel and a favourite with the rich and famous, also overlooks its own splendid 200-year old Moorish garden. The Minzah in Tanger oozes history and intrigue, just a stone's throw from the Grand Socco and medina.

Rabat

Le Marrakech (£)
Painted in bright pastels, the rooms are basic but clean, arranged around a small patio.
✉ 10 rue Sebbahi ☎ 727703, fax 731205

Rabat Chellah (££)
Efficient modern hotel in a quiet residential street close to the museum and city centre. Several good restaurants including 'Le Kanoun' for grills and 'La Medersa' with an international and Moroccan menu.
✉ 2 rue d'Ifni
☎ 701051/701059, fax 706354/731866

La Tour Hassan (£££)
Rabat's most luxurious hotel, centrally located with a pleasant Andalucian garden around the pool.
✉ 26 avenue du Chellah
☎ 723076/721491, fax: 725408

Moyen Atlas and Imperial Cities

Bin el-Ouidane

Auberge du Lac (£)
Simple but charming hotel in these stunning surroundings. Moroccan and European restaurant and a strange but popular bar.
✉ Near the lake, about 30km from Beni Mellal ☎ 5, through the post office of Beni Mellal

Fès

Palais Jamai (£££)
One of Morocco's special hotels, in the splendour of a former palace with stunning views over the medina of Fès el-Bali and surrounding hills. The swimming pool is set in a fragrant Andalucian garden. Breakfast or lunch on the terrace is a must. Good restaurants and a wonderful hammam.
✉ Bab Guissa, Fès el-Bali
☎ 634331–33, fax 635096

Splendid (£)
Clear to see why this is a popular choice with tour companies: cheap, clean and central, with friendly staff and a small pool.
✉ 9 rue Abdelkrim el-Khattabi
☎ 622148, fax 654892

Meknès

Majestic (£)
Very friendly and characterful old hotel in the centre of the *ville nouvelle* with clean, comfortable rooms (quieter on the inside courtyard).
✉ 19 avenue Mohammed V
☎ 522035, fax 527427

Transatlantique (££–£££)
Quiet, extremely friendly hotel, slightly outside the centre, with two swimming pools, tennis courts and a beautiful garden. The rooms and restaurants have fantastic views over the medina, especially spectacular at night. Rooms in the old part of the building have more character.
✉ rue El-Marinynes, Ville Nouvelle ☎ 525051, fax 520057

Volubilis

Volubilis Inn (££)
A peaceful hotel in well-kept gardens with comfortable rooms and a terrace overlooking the amazing site of Volubilis. A great escape from the nearby cities of Meknès and Fès, and excellent base from which to explore the interesting region of Jbel Zerhoun. Swimming pool and horse-riding.
✉ Route P28, Moulay Idriss, Zerhoun ☎ fax 636393/544369

The High Atlas and The South

Asni

Grand Hotel du Toubkal (£–££)
Delightful, unpretentious hotel with a Moorish dining room. Splendid views over Jbel Toubkal. The pool is often empty. Nice garden.
Main road, Asni ☎ 3 via Marrakech

Erfoud

Auberge-kasbah Derkaoua 'Oasis' (£££)
A few sumptuous rooms in a desert kasbah.
At km23 to Merzouga (► 100) ☎ /fax 577140

Gorge du Todra

Hotel des Roches (£)
Basic, well-kept rooms with hot water. Friendly service.

Marrakech

Gallia (£)
Small but impeccably kept hotel near the Jemaa el-Fna. Rooms look out on a wonderful courtyard where a good breakfast is served. Heating in winter and a few rooms with air-conditioning. Recommended, but book in advance.
30 rue de la Recette
☎ 445913, fax444853

La Mamounia (£££)
The Mamounia is a place of fantasy, offering all the services you would expect from one of the best hotels in the world. Luxurious rooms, more than excellent service, a wonderful breakfast buffet on the terrace and one of Morocco's most beautiful gardens. World-class restaurants (► 101).
avenue Bab el Jedid ☎ 448981, fax 444940/444660

Ouarzazate

Auberge el-Ouidane (£)
Ten very basic rooms (one toilet and cold shower between them), overlooking Aït Benhaddou's kasbah.
Just before Aït Benhaddou

Berbère Palace (£££)
Central garden hotel with Berber-style rooms. Pool, very good restaurants and sports facilities.
quartier Mansour ed-Dahabi
☎ 883077, fax 883071

Ouirgane

Au Sanglier qui Fume (£)
Small hotel in a green wadi, living off its reputation but still retaining some charm.
val d'Ouirgane ☎ 9, via the post office

Taroudannt

La Gazelle d'Or (£££)
Renowned as one of Morocco's best and most exclusive (only 30 rooms), decorated in a tasteful mix of Moroccan and European style, and set in an extraordinary, mature garden. Breakfast is served on your own terrace, with the snowcapped Atlas mountains as a backdrop. Formal dinners.
2km outside Taroudannt
☎ 08-852039, fax 08-852737

Palais Salam (££)
Pretty hotel in the former palace of the governor of Taroudannt. Lovely garden. Comfortable rooms and pool.
Within the walls
☎ 852501, fax 852654

Taroudannt (£)
Beautiful retro hotel with basic clean rooms in real colonial-style. Avoid the noisy streetside rooms.
place Assarag, next to the bus stop ☎ 852416

Zagora

La Fibule du Dra (££)
Twenty comfortable rooms arranged in a lush garden with palm trees and a swimming pool.
2km from the centre
☎ 847318, fax 47271

Hotel Standards
Morocco has been criticised abroad for not using internationally-recognised standards to grade its hotels. Few of its five-star hotels, for instance, came anywhere near international standards, although there were notable exceptions. This is changing: many of the big hotels have improved services and amenities, while the government has sent out its inspectors to look again. In the latest check of 263 hotels, 77 had their status changed. Some, happily, were upgraded.

Arts & Antiques/ Books/Handicrafts

'Faux Guides'
Unofficial guides can make life pretty difficult and unpleasant for visitors. If you ignore them they may become aggressive or try to convince you that the medina is a dangerous place. Nothing is less true: they are the only problem. Try to stay friendly and calm, thank them for their services and hospitality, but no, you have been there before and know your way. To avoid trouble book an official guide from the hotel or tourist office, but remember it is fun to get lost off the main street in the medina and the gateway is never far away.

Art and Antiques

The North

Tanger

Bazar Tindouf
Several shops, opposite the Minzah hotel, stuffed from floor to ceiling with antiques, carpets, paintings and copper ware. Lovely to sniff around but don't expect any bargains.
✉ 64 rue de la Liberté
☎ 931525

Majid
A real treasure cove with several floors full of antique clothes, jewellery, fabrics and furniture. Mr Abdel Majid is always happy to guide you through his treasures and is particularly enthusiastic about his antique fabric collection. Don't miss it!
✉ 66 Zankat El-Mouahidine, off Petit Socco ☎ 938892

The Atlantic Coast

Essaouira

Galerie d'Art Fréderic Damgaard
M Damgaard, long-time resident of Essaouira, encourages and then sells the best of the local Berber painters, most of whose work is colourful and primitive, in his spacious gallery. His mission is to make them better known abroad and some of his protegées are gaining international reputations. M Damgaard is always delighted to show and discuss the work to visitors. Fascinating. Recommended.
✉ avenue Oqba ibn Nafiaa
☎ 784446

Rabat

L'Atelier
The country's best art gallery, run by Madame Demasier, who shows the most important Arab and Islamic art.
✉ 16 rue Annaba ☎ 778164

High Atlas and The South

Marrakech

Antiquaire El-Abidi Nasser Eddine
Beautiful collection of old jewellery, amber, hands of Fatma and heavy Berber necklaces.
✉ 9 Souk Semmarine
☎ 441066

La Lampe d'Aladin
Doors and chests keep on opening with more treasures hidden inside. Large shop with old jewellery, carpets, antiques, Orientalist paintings and objets d'art.
✉ 99 and 70bis Souk Semmarine ☎ 443484

Books

The North

Chechaouen

Librairie Alnahj
Best bookshop in town.
✉ 15 avenue Hassan II

Tanger

Librairie les Colonnes
Good bookshop with a wide selection of books on Tanger and Morocco, mainly in French, but also in several other languages.
✉ 54 boulevard Pasteur
☎ 936955

The Atlantic Coast

Casablanca

English Forum
English language bookshop with a good selection,

including books on Morocco.
✉ **27 rue Clémenceau**

Rabat

Bookshop
Excellent choice of new and second-hand English language books, very well arranged, and a friendly shopowner who loves giving advice.
✉ **7 rue al-Yamama** ☎ **706593**

Moyen Atlas and Imperial Cities

Fès

The English Bookshop
Small selection of English language books and, in spite of its name, in French.
✉ **68 avenue HassanII, near the place de la Résistance, Fès, Nouvelle Ville** ☎ **620842**

Handicrafts and Gifts

The North

Ouezzane

Centre Artisanale
Ouezzane is famous for its carpets which are on sale in the weavers' souk or at fixed prices in one of the Centres Artisanale.
✉ **place de l'Indépendence or avenue Hassan II**

Tanger

Parfumerie Madini
The Madini family has been distilling essential oils for 14 generations. Knowing the secret of perfect combinations, they have listed the millionairess Barbara Hutton and the emirs of Kuwait amongst their many famous customers. Wonderful naturally-perfumed soaps and creams. This tiny shop will soon be on the Internet. A large branch has opened on 14 boulevard Pasteur (shop No 5), downtown.
✉ **14 rue Sebou, Medina of Tanger** ☎ **934388**

Tetouan

Ensemble Artisanal
Local crafts at high fixed prices, so you know the maximum to pay in the souks.
✉ **boulevard Hasan II**

The Atlantic Coast

Casablanca

Coopartim
A good place to look at or buy crafts with an excellent selection and friendly staff. Purchases can be shipped.
✉ **Grande Arcade Commerciale, off place des Nations Unies**

Territoire
Lovely shop selling natural perfumes created by Dominique Champeaux, packaged in elegant coloured glass bottles finished with filigrane work or in thuya wood from Essaouira.
✉ **C.I.L., rue Ain Asserdane** ☎ **394774**

Essaouira

Meeting Musical Carrefour
A good display of musical instruments explaining the four musical influences in Morocco: Berber, Arab, Andalucian and Gnaoui or African.
✉ **rue Youssef ben Tachfine**

Rabat

Ali Bazar
A good choice of Moroccan crafts at reasonable prices.
✉ **10 rue Laghuat, in front of the cathedral**

Complexe Artisanal de Rabat
All the crafts from different regions are on sale here at fixed prices. Artisans have been installed in the courtyard workshops.
✉ **At the foot of the Kasbah des Oudaïas**

Guides
Official guides carry identification from the Ministry of Tourism and work according to fixed prices (usually by the hour). They are cheap. But be warned that even these guides earn a commission when you shop. If you only want to sightsee, then make this clear before you set off. Even then you might find yourself in a carpet shop, 'juste pour le plaisir des yeux', for the pleasure of your eyes...

Maps
Imprimerie Royale, me Ait Ba Amrane (off Boulevard Mohammed V, in Casablanca, ☎ 244445) sells maps on Morocco. Otherwise contact the Tourist Office in Casablanca (▶ 50 for details).

Fata Morgana
Contemporary Moroccan furniture and design objects, inspired by old techniques and craft traditions by Jonathan Amar and other young designers.
✉ **11 rue Tafraout, quartier Hassan**

Safi

Souk des Potteries
Safi pottery is sold all over Morocco, but here you can see it being made. Also a good place to buy the green tiles used everywhere in Morocco.
✉ **Bab Chaaba**

Salé

Complexe Artisanal de Salé
Vast complex with a wide choice of traditional and more modern crafts at prices only slightly higher than in the tourist bazars. Worth a visit.
✉ **On the road to the airport from the centre, leave Marjane to the left and take a right past the railway**

Moyen Atlas

Fès

Berrada
The most celebrated silvershop in Morocco, by appointment to King Hassan II and King Fahd of Saudi Arabia.
✉ **40 boulevard Mohammed V**

Centre Artisanal
One of the most pleasant of the country's artisanal centres, with a good collection of carpets and rugs.
✉ **Next door to the PLM Volubilis Hotel, avenue Allal-Ben-Abdallah**

Chez Fakhari Hamida
A good choice of typical Fès pottery with white and blue designs, in the basement of a pottery workshop.
✉ **quartier des potiers, outside the medina on the left on the road to Taza**

Souk du Henné
Lovely square with trees and fountains where the henna used to colour hands and feet in exquisite patterns for weddings is sold, as well as other natural dyes used in make-up, such as khol (for the eyes).
✉ **Near Dar Saada, Fès el Bali**

Meknès

Palais de l'Artisan
Meknès is famous for ironwork chased with silver thread. This is one of the better workshops.
✉ **Souk Kissariat Lahrir No 11, near the Grand Mosque**

High Atlas and The South

Marrakech

Souk el-Haddadine
In a narrow, black and noisy alley you will find iron workers in their tiny workshops making the lovely gates you see everywhere in Morocco. Also some wild candelabra for the tourist market. A scene from hell.
✉ **West of the Medersa Ben Youssef, off the more obvious Souk du Cuivre**

Ouarzazate

Cooperative Artisanale for carpet weaving
A good place to get an idea of the variety of things on sale, fixed prices.
✉ **avenue Mohammed V, opposite the Gendarmerie**

Ensemble Artisanal
Series of workshops and a good shop with fixed prices selling brightly-coloured *ouzquita* carpets, woven by the tribe of the same name.
Opposite the kasbah de Taourirt

Miloud
One of the best potters with some unusual designs.
Village des Potiers de Marrakech, at el-Fakhara 8km outside the centre on the road to Essaouira

Tiznit

Souk des Bijoutiers
Tiznit is the centre for Berber jewellery so if you are into it, this the place to be. Bargaining can be tough here. Pleasant café just outside.

Markets and Food

The Atlantic Coast

Casablanca

Marché des Olives
Tucked away in a courtyard of the new medina, this is a great place if you like the famous Casablanca olives, a mixture of black and green olives with preserved lemon and herbs. Olives come in all colours and all flavours here and can be tasted and tested.
Quartier Habous

Pâtisserie Bennis
By far the best place for Moroccan pastries, just follow your nose and taste sweet paradise.
2 rue Fkih el-Gabbas, Habous

Vita
The best known florist in town sells a selection of beautiful little palm trees or orange trees.
17 rue Colbert

Moyen Atlas and Imperial Cities

Meknès

Meknès Market
Excellent food market to shop for a picnic or a snack with the best dates in the region and wonderful displays of spices and olives.
Off place el-Hedime

High Atlas and The South

Marrakech

Al-Jawda
Behind a small façade is one of the best pâtisseries in Morocco, Chez Mme Alami. Here again the *cornes de gazelle* alone are worth the journey.
11 rue de la Liberté

Majid
One of many spice sellers who will gladly show you his chameleons, turtles and then of course the wide range of spices and herbs. Ghassoul is dried mud used to thicken your hair. Henna is used to colour the hair and make the designs on hands and feet. Zoac is a terracotta stone drenched in poppies which is used as a lipstick. Musk is used to perfume your wardrobe. All this and more!
place de Rahba-Kedima, medina

Marché Central
Excellent food market where you can also stock up on wine and French cheeses. Baskets and pottery are cheaper than in the souk.
avenue Mohammed V

Spices and More Spices
Morocco is famous for its handicrafts like pottery and woodwork, but spices, all important in Moroccan cuisine, are just as much fun to take home. Spices are cheap and of good quality, and a trip to the spice market is a little adventure for the senses: rosebuds, musk, amber, incense, cumin, saffron, cinnamon, cloves...The whole world within reach. Then there are all the ingredients for the traditional medicine and aphrodisiacs...

Children's Attractions

Baby Care
Morocco's population is young and many of them are having babies, which means that especially in cities and towns, you will easily find locally made disposable nappies and baby food. In the main cities you will also find imported baby products, especially from France, Spain and Italy. Pharmacies usually stock a range of baby lotions, cereals and beakers.

Morocco might not seem an obvious choice, but it can be a great place for children. Moroccans, both men and women, just adore young children, especially babies. They will come up and kiss them, hold them or play games with them, wherever you are, be it on the train, in a restaurant or in the medina. Travelling with children you may have much less trouble with the usual *faux guides* and hustlers, who often seem to respect the fact that you are *en famille*.

As for child-friendly areas: medinas are mostly pedestrian-only, the main danger coming from the occasional stray donkey. Outside the city there are many possibilities for entertaining children with easy walks in the hills, a picnic by a fast river, playing in the snow in the mountains, a swim in a shallow bay of the ocean, a donkey-ride, a paddle in a river or waterfall pool, or a more rigourous adventure...

Having said that, places specifically designed for children are few and far between. Most four- and five-star hotels have either a small paddling pool or a shallow end of a large pool for children and some hotels organize children's activities (check with your travel agent). Some major cities have theme parks, but they tend to get very crowded on holidays and weekends and are not always up to European safety standards. Most zoos are quite small and not very interesting for children used to European zoos.

The Atlantic Coast

Agadir

Vallée des Oiseaux
A small park with a little zoo, bird cages, toy train rides and a childrens' playground laid out in a dry river bed.
✉ boulevard du 20 Août, Agadir ⌚ Daily 9:30–12:30, 2:30–6:30

Casablanca

MacDonalds
The famous chain has arrived in Morocco, and with a small playground beside the ocean, this is where many middle-class Casablancans take their children.
✉ Corniche, Aïn Diab 🚌 Bus 9 from the boulevard de Paris

Sindbad
A large but quite old-fashioned amusement park, marked by a large cut-out of Sindbad pointing inland. Fun for the children, but gets extremely crowded on weekends.
✉ Corniche Ain Diab, near marabout of Sidi Abderrahmane

Oualidia

Oualidia beach
Very spacious beach which is excellent for children, as it leads into a shallow lagoon, protected from the stormy Atlantic.

Tarhazout

Tarhazout beach
Large stretch of beach with very shallow water, excellent for children, although you must watch out for the undertow typical for the Atlantic Ocean (► 54).

Temara

Temara Zoo
By far the best zoo in

Morocco with a large selection of animals, lions, gazelles, desert foxes, jackals, monkeys and a lake with flamingos and pelicans. The animals were formerly part of King Hassan II's private collection.

⊠ 14km south of Rabat
🕐 Daily 9:30–dusk

Moyen Atlas

Barrage and Lac de Bin el-Ouidane

Wonderful place to spend a day picnicking, swimming, walking and sunbathing on the shores of this usually desolate lake (for older children). Near by is the Cascades d'Ouzoud, also popular with families as a day trip.

Meknès

Foire de Meknès

Large funfair with big helterskelter and a huge wheel. Popular at weekends. There is a tourist office in the grounds, so you can work out what to do next...

⊠ esplanade de la Foire

Jardin Zoologique de Haboul

Public gardens just outside the medina, complete with a small zoo and an open air theatre.

⊠ Along the medina walls
🕐 Daily 9–5

Place el-Hedim

The horses on place el-Hedim are there for Moroccan men to have their picture taken in true imperial style, in front of the Bab Mansour, but children can feel like little princes and princesses taking a ride around the lively square.

High Atlas and The South

Marrakech

Jemaa el Fna

Although initially overwhelming to everyone, children love this square, with its exotic entertainments: snake charmers, jumpy monkeys, magicians, fire spitters and loud gnaoui musicians (► 19).

Souk des épices de Rahba Kedima

While you are sniffing out pot pourris and spices, the children will be entertained by holding chameleons, snakes and turtles.

⊠ Medina de Marrakech

Ouarzazate

Jardin Zoologique

Another small, recently established zoo mostly for local kids.

⊠ Near the Zat hotel

The North

Chechaouen

The pedestrian square Uta-el-Hammam is a favourite hang-out for local children who run around and play ball, while their parents watch the world go by from one of the terraces.

Tanger

The Forbes Museum

Children are usually more fascinated than adults by American multi-millionaire Forbes' collection of miniature soldiers on several battlefields. They can usually have a good run in the garden afterwards.

⊠ rue Shakespeare
🕐 Fri–Wed 10–5

Kids on the Road

Morocco has no laws concerning the safety of children in cars, which means that most rented cars and taxis will not have rear seatbelts. If you are renting a car and are concerned about this you will need to confirm in advance that your car will have rear belts (international agencies are no more likely than local ones to be able to provide them) and we recommend that you take your own strap-in seats to Morocco.

Nightclubs & Discos/ Theatres

Hammams

Every medina has at least one hammam (communal steam bath) where you can sweat a few hours away and delight in throwing buckets of cool water over yourself. Professional masseurs offer traditional massage or a scrub with a loofah. Some medinas have separate hammams for women or men, others just have different hours or days for the sexes. Hammams in the Palais Jamai (Fès) and La Mamounia (Marrakech) are fantastically luxurious.

Nightclubs and Discos

The North

Tanger

Borsalino

Up-market meeting place for well-heeled Tangerinos. The owner, dressed in thirties style, personally checks arrivals. It helps to be known and/or well-dressed.

✉ 30 avenue Prince Moulay-Abdallahr 🕒 Best after midnight

Morocco Palace

Very Moroccan atmosphere with Egyptian belly dancers, much cheaper than the Borsalino, often frequented by prostitutes. Strange but fun place, especially late at night.

✉ rue Ahmed Chaouki

Scott's

Mostly gay, though not exclusively, this disco is decorated with bizarre paintings of Berber boys in soldiers uniforms.

✉ rue el-Moutanabbi

The Atlantic Coast

Agadir

Corniche Restaurant Bar

Lively night spot, often with music by good local bands.

✉ Beach front

Disco Tan Tan

One of the better hotel discos. Rather crowded at weekends.

✉ Hotel Almohades, boulevard 20 Août ☎ 840233

Casablanca

Caesar's

More up-market disco with good western music.

✉ Sheraton Hotel, 100 avenue des F.A.R. ☎ 317878

La Fontaine

Popular night-spot/strip joint with lively belly dancers, a stirring Moroccan band and female staff who will insist on being bought expensive drinks.

✉ boulevard Houphouet Boigny

Palm Beach Club

If you get weary of the downtown bars and want something closer to the Casa of the imagination, try this beer hall, where the alcohol flows, belly dancers cavort and the police are outside, ready to sort out fights and over-indulgence.

✉ Ain Diab, on the Corniche

Au Petit Poucet

Attached to the restaurant (► 95) is a serious bar, which attracts its faithful habituées as well as the occasional low-life.

✉ 86 boulevard Mohammed V

Rabat

Amnesia

Popular with Rabat's elite and the city's many foreigners, latest music from Europe.

✉ 18 rue Monastir ☎ 701860

Le Jour et Nuit

African music, lots of young people and a relaxed atmosphere.

✉ avenue du Chellah

Le Kasbah

In a red house on plage Rosemarie, a pleasant disco for the summer as you can go for a stroll on the beach when it all gets too hot. Friday nights are particularly good.

✉ plage Rosemarie on the coastal road Rabat-Casa near the Oued Yquem ☎ 749116

Moyen Atlas and Imperial Cities

Fès

Les Mérenides
Fashionable discothèque, where the rich, young Fassis congregate for their weekend entertainment. Suitably expensive.
✉ **Hotel Les Mérenides, Borj Nord** ☎ **645226**

Meknès

Nightclub
Meeting place for the trendy youth of Meknès, with international music. Completely packed on Saturday evenings.
✉ **Hotel Zaki, boulevard el-Massira, Ville Nouvelle, Meknès** ☎ **520063**

High Atlas and The South

Marrakech

Ancien Casino de Marrakech
Food and folklore show with horsemanship, dance, music etc.
✉ **avenue el-Kadissia**
☎ **448811**

Grand Casino de la Mamounia
Glamorous casino often frequented by the stars, so make sure you dress up for the occasion.
✉ **Hotel La Mamounia (► 101), Marrakech** ☎ **444570**

Paradise
Big discothèque with all the latest in music and equipment – a very popular venue with young Marrakchis.
✉ **Hotel Pullman Mansour ed-Dahabi, avenue de France, Marrakech** ☎ **448222**

Theatres

The North

Asilah

Le Palais de la Culture
A cultural centre in the former residence of the local brigand Ahmed al-Rasouli, generally only open during the International Festival in August.
✉ **Medina**

The Atlantic Coast

Rabat

Théâtre National Mohammed V
A wide range of dramatic productions and music concerts.
✉ **rue el-Kahira**

Moyen Atlas and Imperial Cities

Meknès

Centre Culturel Français de Meknès
Very active centre with a monthly programme of exhibitions, concerts, theatre and mainly French-language films.
✉ **337 zankat Farhat Hachad, off avenue HassanII** ☎ **524071**
🕒 **Closed Aug**

High Atlas and The South

Gueliz

Centre Culturel Français de Marrakech
Regular films, concerts, exhibitions and a pleasant garden.
✉ **route de la Targa**

Marrakech

American Language Center
Weekly film.
✉ **3 Impasse Moulin du Gueliz**

Fantasias
During the moussems or festivals, you can watch Moroccan popular culture at its best, with music, singing, dancing and horse-riding. The fantasia is often the highlight with horses galloping while the riders fire their guns. One of the most spectacular fantasias is held during the moussem of Ben Aissa in Meknès (on the birthday of Prophet Mohammed). Fantasias for tourists are staged quite successfully in Marrakech, particularly in the tents on the Casablanca road.

Sports

Golf Courses
King Hassan II is a fervent golfer and believes that golf tourism has a big future in his country. There are now 14 excellent golf courses in the main cities, often in prime locations, and that number is set to rise to 30 by the end of the century. Morocco's major competitions attract golfers from around the world, the most prestigious being the Hassan II Trophy held at the Royal Dar-es-Salam Golf Course, Rabat. Information from the Royal Moroccan Golf Federation ☎ 755636, fax 751026.

The North

Bird-watching

As the Straits are the easiest crossing between Europe and Africa, Tanger is an excellent place to watch birds migrate, north in spring and south in the autumn.

Merdja Zerga
Lagoon and wetland area which is perfect for bird-watching all year around. Plenty of flamingos, marsh owl, black-winged stilts, gulls and black tern amongst many others.
✉ **Near Moulay Bousselham**

Golf

Royal Golf de Tanger
18 hole. 5,529m. Par 72.
✉ **Boubana, Tanger**
☎ **938925**

Tennis

M'Sallah Garden Tennis Courts
✉ **rue de Belgique, Tanger**
☎ **935203**

Yachting

Tanger Yacht Club
✉ **Port** ☎ **938575**

The Atlantic Coast

Football

Stade Marcel Cédan
The best place in Morocco to watch football matches. (Check local papers for details.)

Golf

Royal Golf d'Anfa
Very prestigious golf course with 9 holes, 2,710m, par 35.
✉ **Hippodrome d'Anfa, Casablanca** ☎ **365355**

Royal Golf de Mohammedia
With 18 holes this is one of the best in the country: 5,917m – par 72.
✉ **25 km north of Casablanca. By the sea** ☎ **324656**

Royal Golf de Rabat
Red: 18 holes, 6,702m – par 73. Blue: 18 holes, 6,205m – par 72. Green: 9 holes, 2,170m – par 32.
✉ **Dar es-Salam, Rabat**
☎ **755864**

Surfing

Surfing Federation
✉ **Harbour of Casablanca**
☎ **259530, fax: 236385**

Windsurfing

Good beaches for windsurfing are Dar Bouazaah, a few kilometres south of Casablanca, Oualidia, Sidi Bouzid near Safi and Diabat and Sidi Kaouiki near Essaouira.

Moyen Atlas and Imperial Cities

Horse-riding

The Volubilis Inn (► 104) has several horses to explore the lovely countryside of Jbel Zerhoun and the site of Volubilis.

Spa

Sidi Harazem Spa
Quite neglected but still popular thermal baths.
✉ **Hotel Sidi Harazem, near Fès** ☎ **690072, fax 690072**

Walking

Jbel Tazzeka National Park
Beautiful walks in outstanding mountain scenery. Can only be reached with own transport.
✉ **Just south of Taza**

White-water Sports

Descent of the Oum er-Rabia river at 60km an hour or some other rivers in the region.

✉ Information: Royal Moroccan Federation of Canoeing, avenue Ibnou Sina, BP332, Rabat ☎/fax 02-770281

High Atlas and The South

Excursions

Camel excursions in Zagora

Hotel La Fibule du Dra organizes camel trips into the desert. **✉** **(► 107)**

Football

Stade al-Harti

Where one of Morocco's star football clubs plays, the Kawkab (KACM).

✉ rue Moulay el-Hassan, Hivernage, Marrakech

Golf

Royal Golf Club

Large 18-hole, 4,805m – par 72.

✉ 6km on the Ouarzazate road, Marrakech ☎ 443441

Horse-riding

Club de l'Atlas

Good horse-riding.

✉ Quartier de la Menara, Marrakech

La Gazelle d'Or

Excellent horses for walks through the countryside and lovely orchards.

✉ **(► 105)**

Ouirgane

The Hotel La Roseraie offers good riding trips in the area for a day or for much longer periods.

☎ 432094, fax 432095

Hunting

For information on hunting boar or other animals in the High or Moyen Atlas, contact Club de la Gazelle de la Chaouia, 21 rue d'Oudin le Romon (☎ 252911).

Skiing

Oukaïmeden

Pleasant ski resort, two hours drive from Marrakech, with the best skiing in Morocco. Snow from February until early April, sometimes longer. There are good-value chalet hotels, seven piste runs, equipment, instructors and an impressive ski-lift at 3,273m. Off-piste skiing is becoming increasingly popular in the Toubkal massif, but so far there are no organised facilities.

Tennis

Most up-market hotels have tennis courts and equipment for hire.

Royal Tennis Club de Marrakech

Eight courts.

✉ Jnane el Harti rue Oued el-Makhazine ☎ 431902

Trekking

One of the most popular trekking excursions in Morocco is to climb Jbel Toubkal (► 18), but it is not to be undertaken carelessly. Only experienced climbers with ice equipment should attempt the peak when it is under snow (Nov–Jun), but the lower routes are easily accessible all year. Information is available from: the Mountain Information Centre of the Ministry of Tourism, 1 rue Oujda, Rabat (☎ 77701280).

Swimming

There are public swimming pools in most towns, but standards of cleanliness are not always very high. Most four- and five-star hotels have good pools, which can usually be used by non-residents for a fee.

What's On When

National Holidays
On national holidays all banks, offices and most shops will be closed for the day.
January 1 New Year's Day
March 3 Throne Day (see below)
May 1 Labour Day
July 9 The King's birthday
August 14 Allegiance Day
November 6 Green March
November 18 Independence Day

Popular Festivals
These smaller moussems are mostly harvest festivals to celebrate the arrival of new crops or rest periods on the agricultural calendar. Most of them involve several days of celebrations with music, dancing, a fair and of course plenty of food and drink.

February
Almond Festival, Tafraout

March
Throne Day is the most important National Holiday with celebrations, parades and fireworks across the country, even in the smallest hamlets

May
Rose harvest festival, Kelaa M'Gouna
Festival of Wax, Salé (► 39)

June
Desert symphonies, Ouarzazate
Cherry festival, Sefrou
Festival of Folk Art, Marrakech

July
Camel festival, Guelmime

August
Cultural festival, Asilah
Asilah International Festival

September
Fiancée-wedding festival, Imilchil (► 39)

October
Date festival, Erfoud
Festival of Sacred Music, Fès

November
Date festival, Erfoud

December
Agadir festival

Religious Festivals
Religious festivals follow the Islamic calendar, which is a lunar calendar, so the dates shift each year (check with the Moroccan Tourist Board).
Ramadan, the month of fasting, is carefully observed by Moroccans (► 39) who abstain from food, drink, cigarettes and many other pleasures from sunrise to sunset. Non-Muslims do not have to observe it, but it is tactful to observe the fast in public by abstaining from smoking or drinking.
Aid es-Segrir celebrates the end of Ramadan. In villages it is mostly a family affair, with everything closed for two days, but in places like Marrakech there are more public festivities.
Aid el-Kebir, the remembrance of Abraham's sacrifice of his son, is celebrated everywhere by the slaughtering of sheep for those who can afford it. Public transport is packed for days before and after the Aid, as people return to spend the holiday with their families. There is no public transport on the day itself.
Moharem, three weeks later is the Muslim New Year, celebrated in the family.
Mouloud is the birthday of Prophet Mohammed, which is also observed nationwide, but usually within the family.
The most 'Moroccan' of all religious festivals are the many *moussems*, held in honour of local *marabouts* (saints). Among the most famous are Moulay Idriss (Zerhoun), the Marriage Moussem (Imilchil), Ben Aissa in Meknès and Wax Candle *moussem* in Salé.

Practical Matters

TIME DIFFERENCES

GMT	Morocco	Germany →	USA (NY) ←	Netherlands →	Spain →
12 noon	12 noon	1PM	7AM	1PM	1PM

BEFORE YOU GO

WHAT YOU NEED

- ● Required
- ○ Suggested
- ▲ Not required

	UK	Germany	USA	Netherlands	Spain
Passport/National Identity Card Passport valid for six months	●	●	●	●	●
Visa (check with your Moroccan consulate)					
Onward or Return Ticket	●	●	●	●	●
Health Inoculations & Malaria Pills	○	○	○	○	○
Health Documentation (no reciprocal agreements)	○	○	○	○	○
Travel Insurance	●	●	●	●	●
Driving Licence (national except USA – international)	●	●	●	●	●
Car Insurance Certificate (If own car – Green Card valid)	●	●	●	●	●
Car Registration Document	●	●	●	●	●

WHEN TO GO

Morocco/Rabat

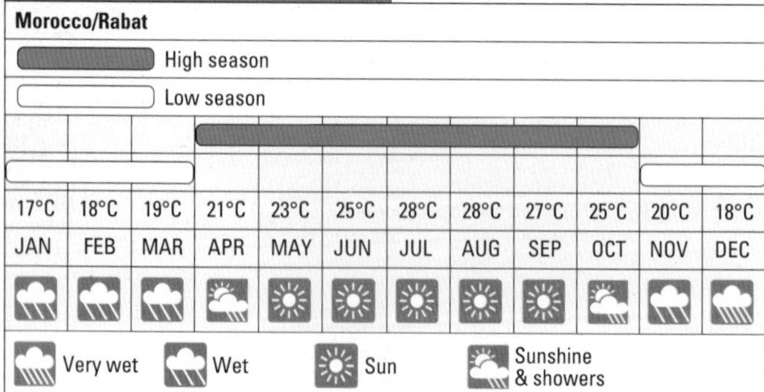

High season

Low season

JAN	FEB	MAR	APR	MAY	JUN	JUL	AUG	SEP	OCT	NOV	DEC
17°C	18°C	19°C	21°C	23°C	25°C	28°C	28°C	27°C	25°C	20°C	18°C

Very wet   Wet   Sun   Sunshine & showers

TOURIST OFFICES

In the UK
Moroccan National Tourist Office
205 Regent Street
London W1R 8BE
☎ 0171 437 0073
Fax: 0171 734 8172

In the USA
Moroccan National Tourist Office
Suite 1201, 20 East 46th Street
New York, NY 10017
☎ 212/557 2520
Fax: 212/949 8148

In Germany
Office National Marocain du Tourisme (ONMT)
Graf Adolf Strasse 59
4000 Dusseldorf 1
☎ (4921) 137 0551/2
Fax: (4921) 137 4048

POLICE 19

FIRE 15

AMBULANCE 15

HIGHWAY EMERGENCY SERVICE 177

WHEN YOU ARE THERE

ARRIVING

The country's national airline, Royal Air Maroc ☎ 0171 439 4361 operates direct, scheduled flights to Moroccan airports from London Heathrow, Paris and other cities in France. New York and Montreal also have direct flights to Morocco. Charter holiday flights are often available from London Gatwick or Heathrow.

Mohammed V Airport, Casablanca

Kilometres to city centre

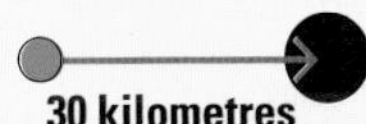

30 kilometres

Journey times

20 minutes

1 hour

1 hour

Marrakech

Kilometres to city centre

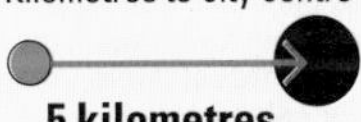

5 kilometres

Journey times

N/A

30 minutes

15 minutes

MONEY

The monetary unit of Morocco is the *dirham*, divided into 100 *centimes*. There are coins for 5, 10, 20 and 50 *centimes* and for 1 and 5 *dirhams*. Notes are issued in 5, 10, 50, 100 and 200 *dirhams*. Currency is labelled in Arabic and French. Keep all exchange slips and budget carefully at the end of your stay, as on departure you will only be allowed to reconvert half of what you can prove to have changed. Eurocheques are accepted in at least one bank in each major city, and both hotels and banks will change cash and travellers' cheques. Credit cards are widely accepted at banks, top hotels, restaurants and shops, but it is wise to check first.

TIME

Morocco stays at Greenwich Mean Time all year, with no Daylight Saving Time in Summer.

CUSTOMS

YES

Alcohol: spirits 1L
Tobacco: 400g *or*
Cigarettes: 200 *or*
Cigars: 50
Perfume: no limit
Toilet water: no limit

You are officially allowed to take one camera, one video camera, one portable typewriter or computer and one radio cassette player with you into the country. If you are driving a car you may import it free for six months, but if you sell it or keep it longer, very high duty will be payable. Even if you write it off you are still obliged to take it out of the country. (This is relevant for all European countries.) Firearms may be imported only with a certificate and a hunting permit which has been obtained before travelling to Morocco.

NO

Narcotic drugs – it is an offence to handle drugs and gaol sentences will be given for those found buying or handling illegal substances. You may not import or export Moroccan currency.

CONSULATES

UK	**Germany**	**USA**	**Netherlands**	**Spain**
731403	709662	762265	733512	704147/8
fax 720906		fax 765661		fax 704694

WHEN YOU ARE THERE

TOURIST OFFICES

Agadir
- place Prince Héritier Sidi Mohammed
  ☎ (08) 84 63 77

Casablanca
- 55 rue Omar Slaoui
  ☎ (02) 27 11 77
  or
- 98 boulevard Mohammed V
  ☎ (02) 22 15 24

Fès
- place de la Résistance
  ☎ (05) 62 34 60

Marrakech
- place Abdelmoumen ben Ali
  ☎ (04) 43 62 39

Meknès
- place Administrative
  ☎ (05) 52 44 26

Rabat
- 22 avenue d'Alger
  ☎ (07) 73 05 62

Tanger
- 29 boulevard Pasteur
  ☎ (09) 93 41 51

In addition to Tourist Offices there are the smaller Syndicats d'Initiative. Both are usually well stocked with colourful local maps and brochures, and will advise you on local transport and dates of the country's major festivals.

NATIONAL HOLIDAYS

J	F	M	A	M	J	J	A	S	O	N	D
2		1		2		1	2			2	

1 Jan	New Year's Day
11 Jan	Independence Manifesto
3 Mar	Feast of the Throne
1 May	Labour Day
23 May	National Day
9 Jul	The King's Birthday (Youth Day)
14 Aug	Allegiance Day
20 Aug	Anniversary of the King's and Peoples Revolution as National Holidays
6 Nov	Day of Green March
18 Nov	Independence Day

In addition, Morocco observes the traditional feast days of the Muslim year, together with Ramadan, the prescribed month of fasting. The dates of these change as they follow the lunar calendar and therefore move backwards by 11 days each year.

OPENING HOURS

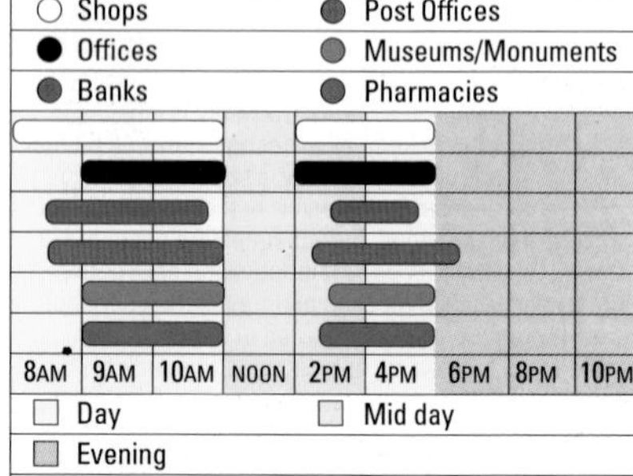

All times given may vary. Many museums are closed on Friday mornings and all day Tuesday.

Banks and offices are closed at weekends.

During Ramadan and in summer, banks are open 8:30–2 and other offices and shops may close early for prayer.

DRIVE ON THE
RIGHT

Try hotels and restaurants
TOILETS
BASIC

PUBLIC TRANSPORT

Internal Flights Royal Air Maroc operates a full schedule of internal flights between the country's principal cities, particularly useful across the huge distances in the Western Sahara and between Tanger and Marrakech. ☎ (02) 912000 Fax: (02) 912397.

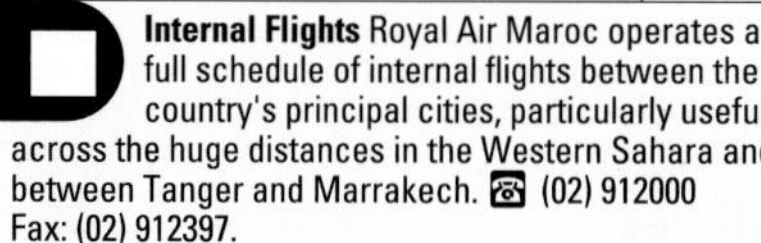

Trains There are essentially two railway lines in Morocco, limited by the physical geography of the country: one from Tanger in the north to Marrakech in the south (due to be extended), and the other between Casablanca and Oujda on the Algerian border. It is worth paying for the air-conditioning in first class in the summer.

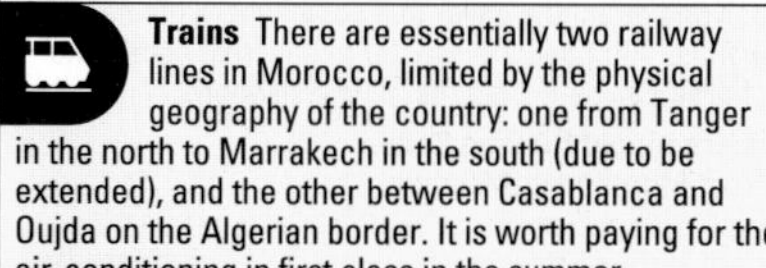

Buses Morocco has a highly competitive bus service: the national bus company CTM, ☎ (02) 449254, runs a fleet of smart modern buses with regular, scheduled services from central bus stations. ONCF, the rail company, runs buses to connect with rail services.

Boat Trips/Ferries Apart from the ferries to and from Morocco and Spain, France and Portugal, there are no 'pleasure' trips. Services between Gibraltar and Tanger run daily and take two and a half hours. These become very overcrowded in summer.

Urban Transport From each central bus station there is a network of local departures covering almost all of the nearby villages. *Petits-taxis* carry up to three passengers around towns and cities – agree a price with driver at start of journey.

CAR RENTAL

Renting is easy but expensive. As well as the international agencies there are also cheaper local firms. Among the best is First-Car: ☎ (02) 31 87 88. Always check you have the vehicle registration certificate and insurance document, and that the spare tyre is in good order.

TAXIS

Grands-taxis and *petits-taxis* are distinguished not only by size but by destination. *Grands-taxis* operate like minibuses, touting for business in the taxi park and driving six passengers at high speed between towns. *Petits-taxis* are confined to towns and cities.

DRIVING

Speed limits on motorways: **120kph**.

Speed limit on all main roads: **100kph**.

Speed limits on urban roads: **40kph**.

By law, drivers and passengers are required to wear seat belts.

No breath-testing, but there are frequent police road-blocks where documents will be checked.

Petrol/gas stations are to be found in towns of any size but are few and far between in rural areas. In remote areas, especially in the south, fill up whenever possible. *Premium* is the standard brand for cars: lead-free is available at large stations. Prices are much in line with Western Europe.

Moroccan mechanics are usually excellent at coping with breakdowns, and all medium-sized towns have garages. If you breakdown miles from anywhere, it will be very expensive to get a lorry to tow you back. Cars must be removed from the country, even if they are a write-off. NB. 21 is the legal driving age in Morocco.

0 1 2 3 4 5 6 7 8
CENTIMETRES

INCHES
0 1 2 3

PERSONAL SAFETY

Travellers may be hassled by guides, often posing as 'students' or 'friends' and extreme caution should be taken in accepting help from these people. Use a guide from the tourist office or manage without. Do not accept offers of cheap hashish. The grey-uniformed *Sûreté* police are normally helpful to tourists.

- Beware pickpockets, especially in crowded places.
- Keep money and passports out of sight.
- Do not walk alone or in medinas at night.
- Women should cover themselves when away from the beach and hotel.

Police assistance:
☎ 19 from any call box

TELEPHONES

Teleboutiques, clearly marked in blue, are plentiful in towns. They give information and change, and are easy to operate, for both international and local calls. Card phones are increasingly available and are also easy to use. The cards can be bought at post offices. Calls can be made from phone offices with operator assistance. The number is given to a telephonist who will dial the call and direct the caller to a cabin where the call is waiting. Although it is simpler to call from hotels, the charge can be double that paid elsewhere.

International Dialling Codes
From Morocco dial 00 then

UK:	**44**
Australia:	**161**
Canada:	**1**
France:	**33**
Germany:	**49**
USA:	**1**
Netherlands:	**31**
Spain:	**34**

POST

All cities and most towns in Morocco have post offices (*PTT*) and although the postal service is reliable, international post can be a little slow. Post to and from Europe can take up to a week, with post to the US, Canada and Australia taking two weeks.
Stamps can be bought at post offices, but in cities and larger towns it is easier to buy them from newspaper and tobacco kiosks. Letters are collected more frequently from post offices so it can help to speed up the service if you post your letters in the box inside or just outside the buildings. Letter boxes are yellow.
Post office opening times are 8–noon and 3–6 Mon–Fri in winter, and 8–3 in summer.

ELECTRICITY

The power supply in Morocco is 220V, although some areas are still on 110V.

Sockets accept two-round-pin plugs and an international adaptor is advisable, and a transformer for appliances operating on 100–120 volts.

TIPS/GRATUITIES

Yes ✓ No ✗		
Restaurants (service incl; tip optional)	✓	7–10%
Cafés/bars	✓	10%
Taxis (negotiate price first)	✓	Change
Museum and site guides	✓	5DH
Car parking *gardien*	✓	2DH
Porters, Chambermaids	✓	5DH
Hairdressers	✓	5DH
Petrol pump attendants	✓	2DH
Toilets (in bars etc)	✓	buy first

PHOTOGRAPHY

What to photograph: Buildings, scenery, street entertainers.
Where you need permission: Many Moroccans dislike being photographed, and it is very unwise to photograph women. Take great care when near military or sensitive installations. Street entertainers expect payment for a picture. Do not photograph children: they will prefer posing to school.
Where to buy film: Film is widely available in Morocco, but purchase only where it has been properly stored or has been recently imported.

HEALTH

Insurance

Morocco has well-qualified doctors in the larger towns and cities and Government hospitals provide free or minimal charge emergency treatment, but full health insurance is essential.

Dental Services

Have a thorough dental check-up before leaving home. Get to a big city and obtain recommendation from a consulate. Dentists will be French-speaking. Medical insurance is essential.

Sun Advice

The sun is very hot. Wear a hat, a high factor sunscreen and drink plenty of bottled water. Avoid too much alcohol and caffeine as these contribute to dehydration, and cover up with light cotton clothes.

Drugs

Though pharmacies are well-supplied, check date stamping as drugs deteriorate quickly in the heat. Drugs are expensive and it is wise to bring a supply of pain-killers, anti-diarrhoea pills and a sun-burn remedy. Do not buy illegal drugs.

Safe Water

Drinking unboiled local water can cause acute stomach problems. Use bottled water and do not eat uncooked food, especially salads washed in local water.
Bilharzia can be caught by swimming in oases or slow-flowing rivers

CONCESSIONS

Students and Youths Student cards are redundant plastic in Morocco. However, Royal Air Maroc do give a 25 per cent discount on their internal flights to people under 26. European InterRail passes for under 26s extend to the Moroccan rail system.

Senior Citizens Winter weather south of Agadir is invariably sunny and the area attracts many retired people. Beach-front hotels offer good rates for long-stay guests, but many do not have lifts or ramps for wheelchairs.

CLOTHING SIZES

Morocco	UK	Rest of Europe	USA	
46	36	46	36	Suits (men)
48	38	48	38	
50	40	50	40	
52	42	52	42	
54	44	54	44	
56	46	56	46	
41	7	41	8	Shoes (men)
42	7.5	42	8.5	
43	8.5	43	9.5	
44	9.5	44	10.5	
45	10.5	45	11.5	
46	11	46	12	
37	14.5	37	14.5	Shirts (men)
38	15	38	15	
39/40	15.5	39/40	15.5	
41	16	41	16	
42	16.5	42	16.5	
43	17	43	17	
36	8	34	6	Dresses (women)
38	10	36	8	
40	12	38	10	
42	14	40	12	
44	16	42	14	
46	18	44	16	
37.5	4.5	37.5	6	Shoes (women)
38	5	38	6.5	
38.5	5.5	38.5	7	
39	6	39	7.5	
40	6.5	40	8	
41	7	41	8.5	

WHEN DEPARTING

- There are no airport taxes, but you should exchange your spare *dirhams* at the airport – it is illegal to import or export Moroccan currency. Have your exchange slips with you, as you are allowed to re-exchange only half of money exchanged.
- Arrive with time to spare at airports and ferry ports, as these are very busy, especially in the summer.
- Owing to civil unrest you should avoid crossing into neighbouring Algeria.

LANGUAGE

The official language of Morocco is Arabic, although 40 per cent of the population still speak Berber dialects. However, Moroccans have a natural linguistic ability and in all but the most rural areas they will also speak French and possibly Spanish. Hotel porters, guides etc can usually be relied upon to know some English. Using a few words of Arabic will give great pleasure. Moghrebi Arabic is a guttural language and hard consonants should be pronounced at the back of the throat, softening them slightly.

English	French	Moghrebi Arabic phonetic pronunciation
a hotel	*un hôtel*	*otel/fondouk*
I want a room	*Je voudrais une chambre*	*B'gheet beet*
Do you have a room?	*Est-ce que vous avez une chambre?*	*Wesh andik wahid beet?*
Can I look at it?	*Est-ce qu'on peut la voir?*	*Wesh yimkin nshoof?*
shower	*la douche*	*doosh*
a bank	*une banque*	*bank*
a post office	*une poste*	*bousta/barid*
too expensive	*trop cher*	*Ghalee bzef*
1 ,2, 3, 4, 5	*un, deux, trois, quatre, cinq*	*wahèd, jooj, tlàta, àrba, khàmsa*
6, 7, 8, 9	*six, sept, huit, neuf*	*sètta, sèba, tmènia, tse'ud*
10, 20, 50	*dix, vingt, cinquante*	*àchra, achrin, khamsin*
100, 1000	*cent, mille*	*mia, alef*
menu (fixed price)	*menu (à prix fixe)*	*ká'ima*
What do you have to eat?	*Qu'est ce que vous avez à manger?*	*Ashmoo kane f'l-makla?*
What do you have to drink	*....à boire*	*....f'l mushahaaroubat*
bread	*pain*	*l'hobs*
salt	*sel*	*l'melha*
water (bottled)	*l'eau (en bouteille)*	*móyyah*
The bill please	*L'addition, s'il vous plait*	*L'h'seb 'minfadlik*
airport	*l'aéroport (m)*	*al-matár*
bus	*l'autobus (m)*	*autobées*
bus station	*la gare routière*	*maháttat al-autobées*
car	*la voiture*	*sayára*
garage	*le garage*	*garáge*
oil (engine)	*l'huile (f)*	*zeit*
petrol	*l'essence (f)*	*benzéen*
puncture	*la crevaison*	*tókob*
yes	*oui*	*eeyeh/wahta*
no	*non*	*la*
please	*s'il vous plaît*	*minfadlik*
thank you	*merci*	*shukran/barakalayfik*
hello (formal)	*bonjour*	*Salam Alaykoom*
hello (informal)	*bonjour*	*labes*
goodbye	*au revoir*	*b'slemah*
excuse me	*excusez-moi*	*smeh lee*
sorry	*pardonnez-moi*	*asif*
good morning	*bonjour*	*sbah l'khir*
go away	*allez vous en!*	*imshi, barra*

INDEX

Acknowledgements
The Automobile Association wishes to thank the following photographers and libraries for their assistance in the preparation of this book.

MAGNUM PHOTOS 11b; MARY EVANS PICTURE LIBRARY 10b; MRI BANKERS' GUIDE TO FOREIGN CURRENCY 119; NATURE PHOTOGRAPHERS 12b (S C Bisserot).
The remaining pictures are held in the Association's own library (AA PHOTO LIBRARY) and were taken by I Burgham F/cover (b) kasbah, F/cover (d) Fes el Bali, 1, 5a, 6b, 7b, 8c, 9b, 9c, 13b, 15a, 15b, 16b, 17b, 18b, 19a, 20b, 21b, 22/3, 23b, 25b, 26b, 30, 33b, 34b, 35, 36b, 36/7, 38b, 39b, 40b, 41b, 42b, 43b, 44, 45, 47a, 48, 49b, 50/1, 54b, 55b, 57, 58b, 59b, 60, 61b, 62b, 63b, 65b, 66/7, 71, 74b, 75b, 76b, 77a, 78b, 79, 80b, 80c, 81c, 82, 83b, 84/5, 87b, 88a, 88b, 89b, 90b, 91a, 91b, 117a, 117b; P Kenwood F/cover (c) dancer, Marrakeck, B/cover Marrakech, Moroccan shoes, 2, 5b, 8b, 13a, 24b, 27a, 27b, 31, 52b, 52c, 53b, 56, 67b, 70, 73, 81a, 86b.

Authors' Acknowledgements
The authors would like to thank the following for invaluable advice and assistance: Mr Ali El Kasmi and Mr El Jaidi at the efficient Moroccan National Tourist Office, London; Mr C Lamriki of Royal Air Maroc, London; John Pointer and TMS PR; Melanie Cutliffe and ZFL PR; Annie Austen; Morocco Made to Measure; Mr Frederick Damgaard; Ingeborg, Titoff and Casa Gerard-Steenbeke.

Contributors
Copy editor: Sheila Hawkins **Page Layout:** The Company of Designers **Verifier:** Pip Leahy
Researcher (Practical Matters): Lesley Allard **Indexer:** Marie Lorimer

Dear Essential Traveller

Your comments, opinions and recommendations are very important to us. So please help us to improve our travel guides by taking a few minutes to complete this simple questionnaire.

You do not need a stamp (unless posted outside the UK). If you do not want to cut this page from your guide, then photocopy it or write your answers on a plain sheet of paper.

Send to: **The Editor, AA World Travel Guides, FREEPOST SCE 4598, Basingstoke RG21 4GY.**

Your recommendations...

We always encourage readers' recommendations for restaurants, nightlife or shopping – if your recommendation is used in the next edition of the guide, we will send you a ***FREE*** **AA *Essential* Guide** of your choice. Please state below the establishment name, location and your reasons for recommending it.

____

____

____

____

Please send me **AA *Essential*** ____________________

(*see list of titles inside the front cover*)

About this guide...

Which title did you buy?

AA *Essential* ____________________

Where did you buy it? ____________________

When? m m / y y

Why did you choose an AA *Essential* Guide? ____________________

____

____

____

____

Did this guide meet your expectations?

Exceeded ☐ Met all ☐ Met most ☐ Fell below ☐

Please give your reasons ____________________

____

____

____

continued on next page...

Were there any aspects of this guide that you particularly liked? ________

Is there anything we could have done better? ________

About you...

Name (*Mr/Mrs/Ms*) ________

Address ________

________ Postcode ________

Daytime tel nos ________

Which age group are you in?

Under 25 ☐ 25–34 ☐ 35–44 ☐ 45–54 ☐ 55–64 ☐ 65+ ☐

How many trips do you make a year?

Less than one ☐ One ☐ Two ☐ Three or more ☐

Are you an AA member? Yes ☐ No ☐

About your trip...

When did you book? m m / y y When did you travel? m m / y y

How long did you stay? ________

Was it for business or leisure? ________

Did you buy any other travel guides for your trip?

If yes, which ones? ________

Thank you for taking the time to complete this questionnaire. Please send it to us as soon as possible, and remember, you do not need a stamp (*unless posted outside the UK*).

Happy Holidays!